MUSIC
and
MATERIALS
for
ANALYSIS

An Anthology

JOSEPH K. DISTEFANO
JAMES A. SEARL

East Carolina University

Ardsley House, Publishers, Inc.

New York

Address orders and editorial
correspondence to:
Ardsley House, Publishers, Inc.
320 Central Park West
New York, NY 10025

ISBN: 1-880157-19-5

Printed in the United States of America

10 9 8 7 6 5 4 3 2 1

From Joe to his mother

From Jim to Anne

Contents

Preface

Music and Materials for Analysis: An Anthology is designed to provide resource material for music theory programs, whether integrated, comprehensive musicianship programs or programs that focus on a single musical element, such as melody, harmony, or form. It can also be used in conjunction with the study of music history. The student must be able to follow a simple line of music visually during its performance. The other basic knowledge needed (for example, scales, intervals, and triads) can be acquired while studying specific compositions in this anthology.

Most of the compositions included here are short, simple works by major composers. This enables the student to perceive the interaction of the various musical elements readily. Some extended compositions are included to permit the application of acquired skills and concepts to more complex works.

Each composition is preceded by a list of *Terms and Concepts* that should be defined in the student's own words and discussed before examining the composition. All of the terms are defined in the *Glossary* at the back of the book. Also preceding each composition are *Study Questions* that not only require application of the foregoing *Terms and Concepts*, but provide a focus for study and analysis. Throughout the anthology, *Study Questions* refer to the *Information Bank* at the back of the book. Contained there are study guides that will help direct the analytical process. Following the *Study Questions*, a section titled *Additional Activities* is frequently included. This section suggests student composition, performance, listening, and research. Manuscript paper is provided with the *Additional Activities* as well as at the back of the book. In conjunction with *Music and Materials for Analysis: An Anthology*, it is recommended that several standard reference works be available for supplementary reading and research (see **Reference Abbreviations**, which follows).

Throughout this anthology, *Study Questions* and *Additional Activities* for a given example will often refer to other compositions. Also, in the *Glossary*, following the definition of a given term the student is often directed to see relevant compositions, other terms, and *Information Bank* references, and supplementary readings that exemplify, enhance, and broaden that term. This cross-referencing and the use of the *Information Bank* enable the student to view compositional procedures common to various periods and styles of music.

Selected compositions are presented chronologically to acquaint the student with various historical techniques, forms, genres, and styles, from medieval monophonic music to twentieth-century music. However, because of the integrated organization of the study materials, the student can perceive common elements that these diverse compositions exhibit.

Initial study can go in any one of several directions. Study may begin with **Example 1** and proceed chronologically, or it can focus on specific musical elements or topics. For example:

(a) Tertian harmony *(Examples 15–21)*

(b) Melody *(Examples 1–5, 8–9, 15–16, 22, 26, 35, 46, and 60)*

(c) Form *(Examples 4–5, 23–25, and 28–30)*

(d) Twentieth-century techniques *(Examples 46–53, 60–61, and 65)*

(e) American music *(Examples 55–59 and 65)*

Additional topics can be devised either by consulting the *Glossary*, where examples are frequently listed following a definition, or by applying to several compositions one or more of the study guides given in the *Information Bank*.

●/●/●/●/●/●/●/●/●/●/●/●/●/●/●/●/●

Acknowledgments

Boulez, *Structures, Ia*, Book I. Copyright 1955 by Universal Edition (London) Ltdf., London. Copyright renewed. All rights reserved. Used by permission of European American Music Distributors Corporation, sole U.S. and Canadian agent for Universal Edition (London) Ltd., London.

Henry Purcell. Lament from *Dido and Aeneas*. As found in: *Expressive Singing, Song Anthology*. Selected, arranged, and edited by Van A. Christy, Vol. 2, Medium Voice Edition. Copyright by Wm. C. Brown Communications, Inc. Used by permission.

Jack Montrose, *A Little Duet for Zoot and Chet*. Copyright 1954. (Renewed 1982) c/o EMI U CATALOG INC. World Print Rights Controlled and Administered by CPP/Belwin, INC, Miami, FL. All Rights Reserved. Used by permission.

Reference Abbreviations

AAM *Analytical Anthology of Music*, 2nd Edition, Ralph Turek, McGraw-Hill, New York, 1992.

BURK *Anthology for Musical Analysis*, 5th Edition, Charles Burkhart, Holt, Rinehart and Winston, New York, 1994.

HAM *Historical Anthology of Music*, Revised Edition, ed. Willi Apel and Archibald T. Davison, Harvard University Press, Cambridge, MA., 1977.

HWM *History of Western Music*, 4th Edition, Donald J. Grout, W. W. Norton, New York, 1988.

MM *Masterpieces of Music Before 1750*, First Edition, Carl Parrish and John F. Ohl, W. W. Norton, New York, 1952.

MTTM *Materials and Techniques of Twentieth-Century Music*, First Edition, Stefan Kostka, Prentice Hall, Englewood Cliffs, NJ., 1990.

Examples 1–3
GREGORIAN CHANT

Kyrie
Agnus Dei
Communion

Terms and Concepts

In your own words, define the following *Terms and Concepts*. When necessary, refer to the *Glossary* at the back of the book.

Antiphon

Articulation

Cadence

C clef

1

Contour

Dynamics

Form

Gregorian chant

Interval

Mass

Melody

Modes, melodic

Neumes

Ordinary

Phrase

Proper

Range

Rhythm

Tempo

Ternary form

Tessitura

Texture, monophonic

Through-composed

Study Questions

1. Compare the stylistic features of these melodies to those in *Examples 4–5, 8–9, 15–16, 25, 35, 46, 58,* and *60.* (See *Information Bank, Topic 2.**) What similarities do you find? How have melodic concepts changed throughout history?

2. Review the eight medieval melodic modes. What are their names? Consider the following points in relation to *Examples 1–3:*
   (a) The distinguishing features of the authentic and plagal (*hypo*) modes
   (b) The intervallic organization of each mode
   (c) The final (tonic) and reciting tone of each mode
   (d) The intervallic relationship of each mode to the major and minor scales

---

*The *Information Bank* is located at the back of the book.

3. How do pitch materials, range, final (tonic), and tessitura help to determine which mode is being used?

4. Locate the cadences in each of these compositions. Which mode (scale) pitches are used at the end of each phrase? How do the cadential pitches help to define the mode of each example? How are these cadential pitches reflected in the music of the Baroque and Classical periods? (For reference, see *Examples 15–16* and *25*.)

5. Define and discuss the following terms in relation to *Examples 1–3*:

    (a) Mass
    (b) Proper
    (c) Ordinary
    (d) Neume
    (e) Trope
    (f) Antiphon
    (g) Performance instructions: ij., iij., asterisk (*), custos (guide note)
    (h) Phrase instructions (barring): quarter, half, full, double

6. Ternary and through-composed are two formal structures used in medieval sacred music. (See *Information Bank, Topics* 4 and 5.) Which of these structures is used in *Example 1*? in *Example 2*? in *Example 3*?

7. Compare the notation on the four-line staff with modern notation. What observations can you make about note values, neume shapes, and order of pitches in a compound neume? Which clef is used on the four-line staff? Compare the four-line notation of each example to its transcription. How is the octave placement effected by an 8 below the G clef?

Additional Activities

1. Using modern notation, compose a short melody for your instrument (or voice) in each of the four authentic modes (Dorian, Phrygian, Lydian, and Mixolydian). Analyze and perform your compositions. (In addition to the manuscript paper that follows, if necessary, use the manuscript paper provided at the back of the book.)

2. Sing each of the melodic modes and be able to recognize each aurally.

3. Analyze and perform examples of Gregorian chant found in *MM* (Nos. 1–3), *HAM* (Nos. 12–15), *AAM*, and *BURK*.*

*See *Reference Abbreviations* on page xix in the front matter.

Additional Activities • 5

Kyrie

Translation

Lord have mercy. Christ have mercy. Lord have mercy.

Example 1. Kyrie • 7

Agnus Dei

Translation

Lamb of God, who takest away the sins of the world, have mercy on us. Lamb of God, who takest away the sins of the world, grant us peace.

mun-   di: mi-   se-   re-re   no- bis.

A- gnus De-   i,* qui tol-   lis

pecca- ta   mun-   di: do- na no-bis pa-cem.

Communion

Translation

Christ our Paschal lamb is slain, alleluia: therefore let us feast with the unleavened bread of sincerity and truth, alleluia.

Example 3. Communion • 9

Examples 4–5

MEDIEVAL SECULAR MONODY

Le Jeu de Robin
Adam de la Halle (c. 1245–87)

C'est la Fine
Guillaume d'Amiens (13th Century)

Terms and Concepts

In your own words, define the following *Terms and Concepts*. When necessary, refer to the *Glossary* at the back of the book. Begin by reviewing the *Terms and Concepts* for *Examples 1–3*.

Modes, rhythmic

Refrain

Verse

Study Questions

1. Compare the stylistic features of these melodies to those in Examples 1–3, 8–9, 15–16, 25, 35, 46, 58, and 60. (See *Information Bank, Topic* 2.) What similarities do you find? How have melodic concepts changed throughout history?

2. Which melodic mode is used in *Example 4*? in *Example 5*?

3. Which rhythmic mode is used in *Example 4?* in *Example 5?* What one factor determines which rhythmic mode is used? What is the relationship between the text and the chosen rhythmic mode?

4. In *Example 4*, verses 1 and 2 are a refrain. Does *Example 5* have a refrain? Discuss the role of a refrain.

5. If capital letters are used for the music of the refrain and lowercase letters for the music of each verse, the form of *Example 4* is ABaabAB. (See *Information Bank, Topic* 5.) Using this same procedure, what is the form of *Example 5*?

6. Identify the structural principles used in *Example 4* and in *Example 5*. (See *Information Bank, Topic 4*.) Find other compositions in this anthology that demonstrate these principles (for instance, see *Examples 21, 25, 36,* and *52*). Is it possible to cite any composition that does not use at least one of these principles?

Additional Activities

1. Compose several short melodies for your instrument (or voice) using various rhythmic and melodic modes. Analyze and perform your compositions. (In addition to the manuscript paper that follows, if necessary, use the manuscript paper provided at the back of the book.)
2. Listen to several currently popular songs. Which ones have refrains?
3. Write and perform a composition with a refrain.

Le Jeu de Robin

Adam de la Halle

Translation

Chorus: 1 and 6	*Robin loves me, Robin has me.*
Chorus: 2 and 7	*Robin asked me if I will continue to love him.*
Solo: 3, 4, and 5	*Robin bought me a skirt of red material, good and beautiful, with petticoat and belt.*

Example 4. *Le Jeu de Robin* • 15

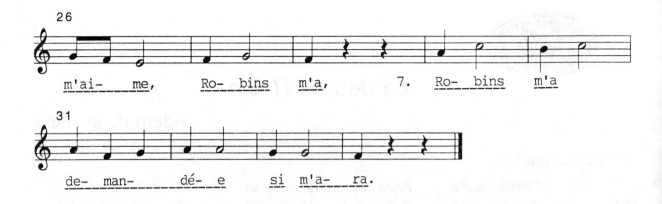

26

m'ai— me, Ro— bins m'a, 7. Ro— bins m'a

31

de— man— dé— e si m'a— ra.

C'est la Fine

Guillaume d'Amiens

Translation

Chorus: 1 and 7	*This is the end, no matter what is said,*
Chorus: 2 and 8	*I shall love.*
Solo: 3	*It is down there amidst the fields.*
Solo: 4	*This is the end, I wish to love.*
Solo: 5	*Games and dances are being held there.*
Solo: 6	*A fair friend have I.*

1

5   1. C'est la   fins,   koi— que nus   di— e,

8 2. J'ai me— rai.   3. C'est la jus en
9
                       4. C'est la fins, je

    mi les pres. 5. Jus et baus   i a le—
14
    veul a— mer. 7. C'est la fins,   koi— que nus

    ves 6. Bele a— mie   ai.
    di— e 8. J'ai me— rai.

Example 6
MOTET

Quam Pulcra Es
John Dunstable (c. 1390–1453)

Terms and Concepts

In your own words, define the following *Terms and Concepts*. When necessary, refer to the *Glossary* at the back of the book.

Cadence

Counterpoint

Fauxbourdon

Motet

Modes, melodic

Musica ficta

Phrase

Texture

Tonal center

Study Questions

1. What is the overall tonal center of this composition? (See *Information Bank, Topic 3.*) What other tonal centers are established?

2. An example of fauxbourdon is found in measure 12. Locate other uses in this composition.

3. Study *Examples 10–11*. Compare these compositions by Palestrina to *Example 6*. Consider the degree of contrapuntal activity, textual treatment, cadences, and clarity of phrases.

4. How does Dunstable achieve unity? What factors supply variety? (See *Information Bank, Topic 1.*)

Additional Activities

1. Read the analysis of *Example 6* in *HWM*.

2. Analyze and perform other music by Dunstable in *HAM* (Nos. 61–62).

Quam Pulcra Es

John Dunstable

Translation

How fair and how pleasant art thou,
oh love, in thy delights.
Thy stature is like to a palm tree,
and thy breasts to clusters of grapes.
Thy head is like Mount Carmel and
thy neck is like a tower of ivory.
Come, my beloved, let us go into the field
and see whether the tender grapes appear
and the pomegranates blossomed.
There will I give thee my loves. Alleluia.

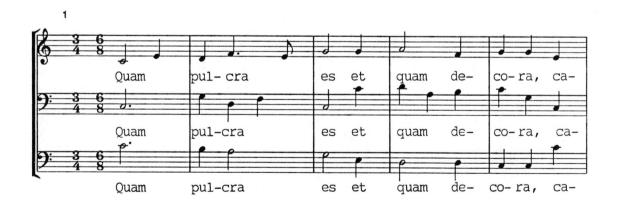

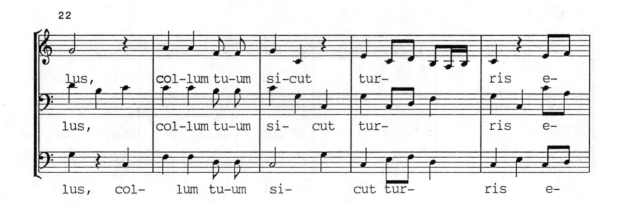

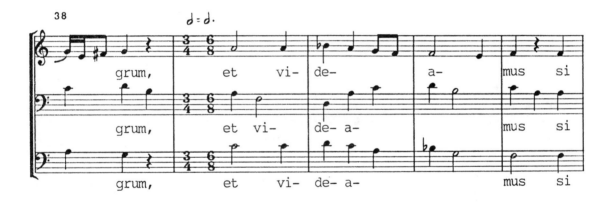

Example 7
MOTET

Ave Christe (Part One)
Josquin des Prez (1440–1521)

Terms and Concepts

In your own words, define the following *Terms and Concepts*. When necessary, refer to the *Glossary* at the back of the book.

Cadence

Consonance

Counterpoint

Dissonance

Imitation

Interval

Inversion, harmonic

Macro rhythm

Micro rhythm

Motet

Nonchord tone

Range

Texture

Tonal center

Triad

Study Questions

1. What is the overall tonal center of this composition? (See *Information Bank, Topic 3*.)
   What other tonal centers are conveyed?

2. Locate the Phrygian cadences. What are the characteristics of each such cadence? What other types of cadence are used?

3. Imitation is used extensively in this composition. Trace its use and identify the different pitches that begin a statement of the same melodic idea. How does the relation of these different pitches help to establish a tonal center and give overall unity to the composition? In what sense is the pitch relationship the same in the fugue of *Example 24*? Also study the imitative procedures used in *Examples 8–11*.

4. A contrast of texture is provided in measures 68–76, *Salve corpus Jesu Christe* ("Hail body of Christ") and measures 90–93, *redemisti* ("redeemed"). For what reasons (other than contrast of texture) is this done?

5. The tenor part in *Example 7* is written with an 8 below the G clef (see *Examples 1–3, 5, 8, 11,* and *12*), which indicates that the tenor sounds an octave lower than written. Therefore, the first pitch in the tenor in *Example 7* is *small b*. What is the range of each voice part in *Example 7*? Use specific pitch nomenclature (see the *HDM* article, "Pitch Names").

6. Before identifying the harmonic dissonance in this example, study *Examples 8–9*. As in those two two-part examples, the dissonant pitch in this four-part example is usually controlled by the lowest-sounding pitch. That is, the harmonic interval that results when each pitch above the lowest is paired with that lowest pitch is either a consonant or a dissonant interval. Therefore, the procedure for identifying dissonance in a

Renaissance four-part composition is to analyze three two-part compositions: bass and tenor, bass and alto, and bass and soprano (assuming that the bass is the lowest-sounding pitch). For example, in measure 16, *small b* in the tenor is a passing tone. As in two-part Renaissance music, when the lowest-sounding pitch is the dissonant pitch (for example, in measure 16, the *small e* in the bass), the harmonic controller is usually the longer note(s) above it. The consonant sonorities in the Netherlands sacred contrapuntal style (*Examples 7–11*) that result from the combination of the individual voices are major and minor triads in either root position or first inversion, the diminished triad in first inversion (rare), and the augmented triad in first inversion (very rare).

When these harmonic procedures are understood, identify the harmonic dissonance in Example 7.

Additional Activities

1. For further study of Josquin's music, see *MM* (No. 19), *HAM* (Nos. 89–91), *BURK*, and *AAM*.

Ave Christe (Part One)

Josquin des Prez

Translation

Hail Christ, sacrificed on the altar of the cross,
hostage of the redeemer, by your death grant that we,
redeemed from the harsh light of day, enjoy with you bright glory.

Hail word, incarnate of the Virgin Mary,
living bread of the Angels,
salvation and hope of the weak, comfort of the sinners.

Hail body of Christ, who from heaven did descend,
and redeemed his people, who on the cross did hang.

Good Jesus, fountain of piety, pride of the angels,
glory of the saints, hope of the sinners,
have mercy on us.

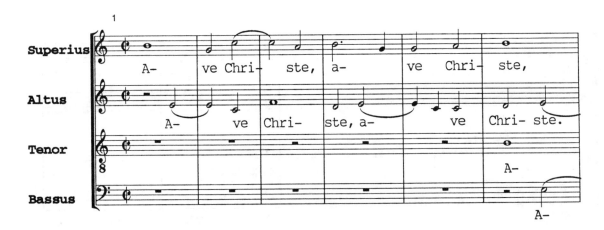

28 • Example 7. Motet: Prez

32 • Example 7. Motet: Prez

Examples 8–9
TWO-PART RESPONSES

Benedictus
Beatus Vir
Orlando Lassus (1532–94)

Terms and Concepts

In your own words, define the following *Terms and Concepts*. When necessary, refer to the *Glossary* at the back of the book.

Consonance

Counterpoint

Dissonance

Imitation

Inversion, melodic

Macro rhythm

Micro rhythm

Modes, melodic

Nonchord tone

Phrase

Pitch names

Range

Study Questions

1. Compare the stylistic features of these melodies to those in *Examples 1–5, 15–16, 25, 35, 46, 58,* and *60.* (See *Information Bank, Topic 2.*) What similarities do you find? How have melodic concepts changed throughout history?

2. The key of an eighteenth-century tonal composition is usually the tonality that is established at the outset and at the conclusion. (See *Information Bank, Topic 3.*) The mode of a Renaissance composition is also usually established at the beginning and at the final

cadence. Which pitches of a particular mode best help to define the tonic (final) of a mode? Also, the cadences, initial pitch of each imitative phrase, and voice ranges usually suggest a specific mode. Indicate the mode of *Example 8* and the mode of *Example 9*.

3. How does chromaticism tend to change the character of the diatonic modes? Compare *Example 9* to *Example 1*, both of which may be considered in the same mode. How does the use of chromaticism anticipate the rise of the major/minor scalar system?

4. Trace the use of imitation in *Example 8* and in *Example 9*. What contrapuntal device is used at the beginning of *Example 9*?

5. The tenor part in *Example 8* is written with an 8 below the G clef (see *Examples 1–3, 5, 7, 11*, and *12*), which indicates that the tenor sounds an octave lower than written. Therefore, the first pitch in the tenor is middle c. What is the range of each voice part in *Example 8*? in *Example 9*? Use specific pitch nomenclature (see the *HDM* article, "Pitch Names").

6. The control of harmonic dissonance is an important element of style in sixteenth-century music. It not only helps provide momentum and direction but also adds

interest and variety. The consonant harmonic intervals in Renaissance sacred music (*Examples 7–11*) are the perfect prime (unison), major and minor third, perfect fifth, major and minor sixth, and perfect octave. All other intervals are treated as dissonance; that is, one of the pitches of the dissonant interval requires resolution to a consonance. This need for resolution necessitates continuation and aids the aforementioned momentum and direction. Analyze the harmonic intervals in *Examples 8* and *9* to determine which intervals are consonant and which are dissonant. That is, the presence of dissonance is determined *vertically* (harmonically). In a harmonic dissonant interval, only one of the two pitches is analyzed as the dissonance—only one requires resolution. The specific name given to the dissonant pitch (passing tone, suspension, and so on) is determined by how it is approached and resolved; that is, it is determined *horizontally* (melodically). When determining which one of two pitches is the dissonant pitch, it will usually be the shorter of the two notes or the note that resolves first.

Additional Activities

1. For further study of Lassus two-part writing, see *BURK* and *AAM*.

Benedictus

Orlando Lassus

Translation

 Blessed is he who cometh in the name of the lord.

Beatus Vir

Orlando Lassus

Translation

Blessed is the man who shall continue in wisdom and who shall meditate in his justice and, in his mind, think of the all-seeing eye of God.

Example 9. Beatus Vir • 37

Examples 10–11

MASS MOVEMENTS

Gabriel Archangelus, **Benedictus**
Ad Fugum, **Benedictus**
Giovanni Pierluigi da Palestrina (1525–94)

Terms and Concepts

In your own words, define the following *Terms and Concepts*. When necessary, refer to the *Glossary* at the back of the book.

Accent

Cadence

Canon

Counterpoint

Dissonance

Imitation

Macro rhythm

Meter

Micro rhythm

Modes, melodic

Nonchord tone

Range

Texture

Study Questions

1. In which melodic mode is *Example 10* written? *Example 11*? Consider the cadences, the first notes of each imitative phrase, and the consistent use of B♭ in *Example 10* before making a decision.

2. In *Example 10*, the alto parts are in canon. To what extent is this contrapuntal device used in *Example 11*? Is this same device used between the *cantus* ("soprano") and the alto I in *Example 10*?

3. How does the use of agogic accents in each melodic line contribute to the independence of each line and to an overall impression of continuous motion? To what extent do the bar lines of each voice part in this modern edition coincide with the agogic accents?

4. The tenor part in *Example 11* is written with an 8 below the G clef (see *Examples 1–3, 5, 7, 8,* and *12*), which indicates that the tenor sounds an octave lower than written. Therefore, the first pitch in the tenor of *Example 11* is d^1. What is the range of each voice part in *Example 11*? Use specific pitch nomenclature (see the *HDM* article, "Pitch Names").

5. For suggested procedures to use when analyzing Renaissance harmonic dissonance, see Study Question 5 of *Example 7* and Study Question 6 of *Examples 8–9*. Apply these analytical procedures to *Examples 10–11*.

6. Discuss the factors that contribute to the selection of a tempo for a given composition. (See *Information Bank, Topic 6*.) Based on this discussion, select a tempo for *Example 10* and for *Example 11*. Are these the same factors used to select a tempo for *Example 12*?

Additional Activities

1. Analyze and perform other music by Palestrina in *HAM* (Nos. 140–141), *MM* (No. 24), *BURK,* and *AAM*.

2. Compose a Dorian melody in $\frac{4}{4}$ meter that conveys micro rhythm. Reinsert bars for the melody so that each agogic accent becomes the first beat of each measure in order to exhibit a multimetric structure. (See *Example 64.*) Perform the melody, first in $\frac{4}{4}$ meter and then with the bars reinserted. Which metric organization produces the better performance? (In addition to the manuscript paper that follows, if necessary, use the manuscript paper provided at the back of the book.)

Gabriel Archangelus
Benedictus

Giovanni Pierluigi da Palestrina

Translation

Blessed is he that cometh in the name of the Lord.

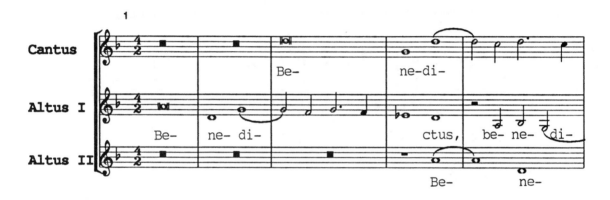

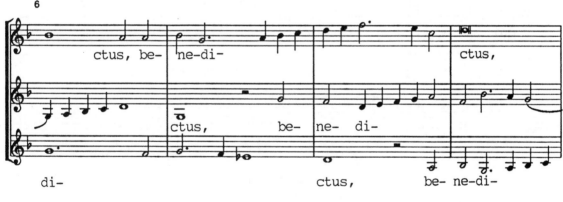

Example 10. *Gabriel Archangelus.* Benedictus • 43

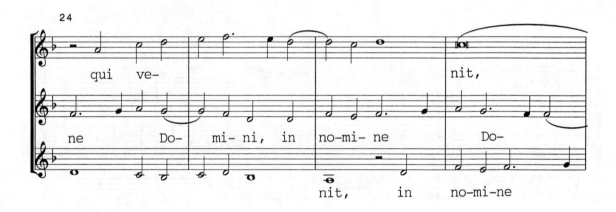

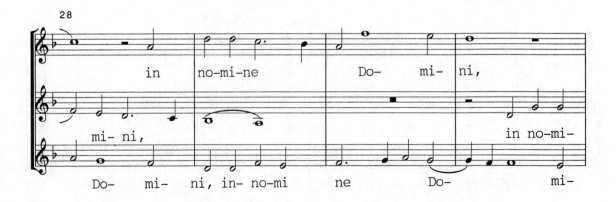

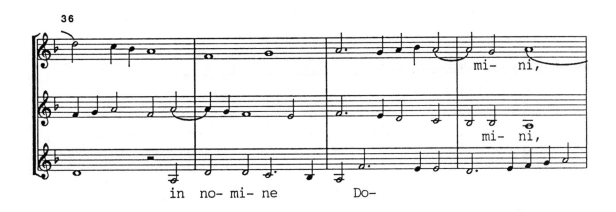

Example 10. *Gabriel Archangelus.* Benedictus • **45**

Ad Fugum
Benedictus

Giovanni Pierluigi da Palestrina

Translation

Blessed is he that cometh in the name of the Lord.

Example 12
BALLETT

Sing We and Chant It
Thomas Morley (1557–1602)

Terms and Concepts

In your own words, define the following *Terms and Concepts*. When necessary, refer to the *Glossary* at the back of the book.

Accent

Ballett

Binary form

Dissonance

Mode, melodic

Nonchord tone

Range

Triad

Study Questions

1. In which mode is *Example 12* written? (See *Study Question 2* of *Examples 1–3*.) Which major scale is equivalent to this mode? Does this composition have more of a tonal or a modal sound?

2. Compare

    (a) the types of chords,

    (b) the harmonic progressions (*root relationships*),

    (c) the part-writing procedures (*voice leading*), and

    (d) the frequency and treatment of dissonance

in this composition to those found in the Bach chorales (see *Examples 15–21*).

3. Read each phrase of the text. How does Morley treat the syllable he considers to have the greatest accent? Compare the treatment of accented syllables in this composition to that used in *Examples 8–11*.

4. Are the bar lines in this example more valid and helpful in performance than those in *Examples 8–11*? Discuss.

5. The tenor part in *Example 12* is written with an 8 below the G clef (see *Examples 1–3, 5, 7, 8,* and *11*), which indicates that the tenor sounds an octave lower than written. Therefore, the first pitch in the tenor of *Example 12* is d¹. What is the range of each voice part in *Example 12*? Use specific pitch nomenclature (see the *HDM* article, "Pitch Names").

6. Discuss the factors that contribute to the selection of a tempo for this composition. (See *Information Bank, Topic 6.*) Based on this discussion, select a tempo. Are these the same factors used to select a tempo for *Examples 10–11*?

Additional Activities

1. Write or select a poem that lends itself to a musical setting. Compose a melody for this poem that conveys the accents of the text through the use of agogic accents in the music. (In addition to the manuscript paper that follows, if necessary, use the manuscript paper provided at the back of the book.)

2. Compose a modal melody. Perform this melody in several different modes by changing only the key signature. Which mode best suits your melody?

Sing We and Chant It

Thomas Morley

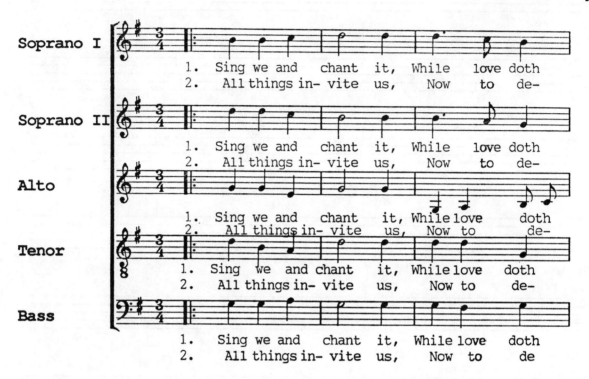

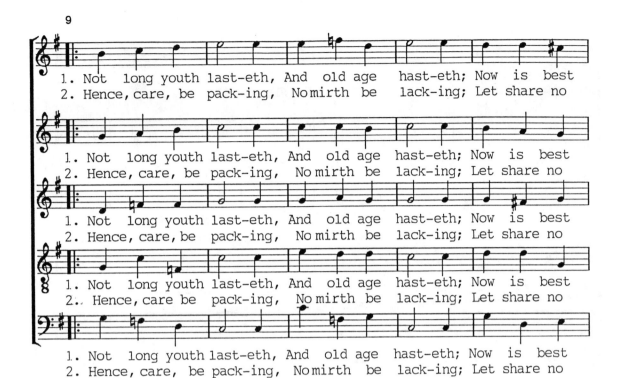

Example 13

RECITATIVE AND ARIA

Dido and Aeneas, Lament
Henry Purcell (c. 1659–95)

Terms and Concepts

In your own words, define the following *Terms and Concepts.* When necessary, refer to the *Glossary* at the back of the book.

Aria

Binary form

Ground bass

Motive

Recitative

Seventh chord

Text painting

Triad

Variation Forms

Study Questions

1. The pairing of a recitative and an aria (the latter begins at measure 9 in this composition) is one of the most frequent couplings in Baroque music. Compare the two. Is it possible to draw parallels between the pairing of the recitative and aria and that of the prelude and fugue (see *Example 24*)?

2. Locate the ground bass at the outset of the aria and trace its subsequent use. How many statements are presented during the entire aria?

3. What form is conveyed by the text and melody of the aria? by the ground bass? (See *Information Bank, Topics 4–5.*)

4. Two important features of this ground bass are its overall descending character and a two-note, chromatically descending motive. Cite derivatives of these features in the vocal line.

5. How is text painting achieved on words and phrases such as "laid in earth," "trouble," and "remember me"?

6. In Baroque, as in Renaissance compositions, diminished chords are sometimes used for text-painting purposes. Locate the diminished triads, half-diminished seventh chords, and fully diminished seventh chords. What factors within these chords contribute to their unstable character? Do these chords help the listener experience the sorrow of the text?

7. Another example of text painting is the depiction of impending death as expressed in the descending and chromatic vocal line of the recitative. Where in the aria are these two melodic characteristics used to express the lamenting text?

Additional Activities

1. Study other ground-bass compositions in *MM* (No. 38), *BURK*, and *AAM*.

2. Compose a ground-bass composition. (In addition to the manuscript paper that follows, if necessary, use the manuscript paper provided at the back of the book.)

Dido and Aeneas
Lament

Henry Purcell

Thy hand, Bel- in - da! Dark - - ness shades me, On thy

bos - som let me rest, More I would,___ but death___ in -

vades me; Death___ is now___ a wel - come___ guest.

• Example 13. Recitative and Aria: Purcell

wrongs___cre - ate   no trou - ble,   no   trou - ble in thy___

breast.   Re - mem-ber me,   re -

mem - ber me,   But ah!_____ for - get   my

fate;   Re - mem-ber me, but ah!_____ for - get   my fate; Re -

Example 14
TRIO SONATA

Op. 4, No. 7
Corrente
Arcangelo Corelli (1653–1713)

Terms and Concepts

In your own words, define the following *Terms and Concepts*. When necessary, refer to the *Glossary* at the back of the book.

Binary form

Cadence

C clef

Continuo

Figured bass

Imitation

Inversion, harmonic

Motive

Nonchord tone

Rounded binary form

Seventh chord

Tonal center

Triad

Trio sonata

Study Questions

1. Discuss the C clef and its various placements on the staff. (See *Examples 43* and *63.*)

2. In which key does the composition begin and end? What tonalities are conveyed by the internal cadences? (See *Information Bank, Topic 3.*)

3. How many instruments are required to perform this composition? Which instruments could be used?

4. Trace the use of imitation in this composition as a device to give unity and variety. (See *Information Bank, Topic 1*.) Identify the motives, and discuss their structural importance.

5. Study the composition as an example of binary form. Compare the structure of this composition to *Examples 26* and *36*. Locate other compositions in binary form in this anthology.

6. What is the purpose of the numbers below each score? Which performer uses this musical "shorthand"?

7. Using the given figured bass, provide a harmonic analysis of *Example 14* and identify its nonchord tones.

8. In the *b* (second) section, what type of dissonance is used in measures 7 and 9 of the top line? When and where is this dissonance resolved?

Additional Activities

1. Supply figured-bass numbers for *Examples 15* and *16*.

2. In a melodic and a harmonic style of your choice, write a composition that includes one or two solo parts with a chordal accompaniment. (In addition to the manuscript paper that follows, if necessary, use the manuscript paper provided at the back of the book.)

3. Study other compositions with figured basses in *MM* (No. 39), *AAM*, and *BURK*.

Op. 4, No. 7
Corrente

Arcangelo Corelli

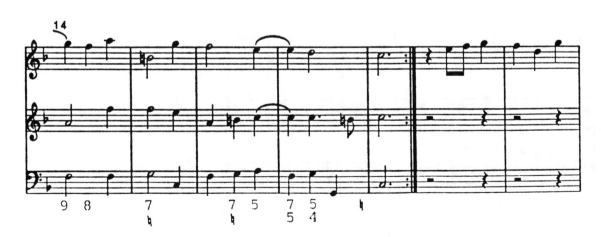

68 • Example 14. Trio Sonata: Corelli

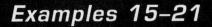

Examples 15–21

Chorale Harmonizations

Johann Sebastian Bach (1685–1750)

Lord Jesus Christ, the Prince of Peace
O Darkest Woe! Ye Tears That Flow
If God Withdraweth, All the Cost
O Lord! How Many Miseries
My Cause Is God's, and I Am Still
O Thou, of God the Father
Blessed Jesu, at Thy Word

Terms and Concepts

In your own words, define the following *Terms and Concepts*. When necessary, refer to the *Glossary* at the back of the book.

Augmented sixth chord

Bar form

Cadence

Chorale

Consonance

Dissonance

Harmonic rhythm

Inversion, harmonic

Modulation

Nonchord tone

Period

Phrase

Secondary chord

Seventh chord

Tertian harmony

Through-composed

Triad

Study Questions

1. Compare the stylistic features of these melodies to those in *Examples 1–5, 8–9, 25, 35, 46, 58,* and *60.* (See *Information Bank, Topic 2.*) What similarities do you find? How have melodic concepts changed throughout history?

2. Perform each chorale, and determine the opening and closing key (overall tonality), phrase structure, and overall form. (See *Information Bank, Topic 3.*)

3. Name the root of each chord, and identify the type of chord used (major triad, minor triad, or dominant seventh, for example).

4. Certain root movements are associated with and help to define major/minor tonality, the primary means of harmonic organization during the eighteenth and nineteenth centuries. Tabulate the root movement of successive chords in *Examples 15–21* (major second up, perfect fourth up, down a minor third, and so on). Which root movements are frequently used? Which are sparingly used?

5. Provide a harmonic analysis of each chorale. Use Roman numerals or other appropriate symbols. Indicate the inversion of each chord. Which chords function as secondary dominant or secondary leading-tone chords? As you encounter each modulation, indi-

cate its type (common chord, chromatic, or phrase). What observations can you make about the harmonic rhythm?

6. Locate and name all of the nonchord tones (see Study Question 6 of *Examples 8–9* for an explanation of how to determine and assign specific names to dissonant pitches). Is it possible to analyze certain pitches as either chord or nonchord tones? For example, analyze the first measure of *Example 16*, the eighth-note *e* in the alto voice.

Additional Activities

1. Choose one of the chorales, and arrange it for instruments. Perform each arrangement. (In addition to the manuscript paper that follows, if necessary, use the manuscript paper provided at the back of the book.)

2. Select one of the chorale melodies (or compose your own), and harmonize it in a style of your choice.

Lord Jesus Christ, the Prince of Peace

Johann Sebastian Bach

O Darkest Woe! Ye Tears That Flow

Johann Sebastian Bach

Example 16. *O Darkest Woe! Ye Tears That Flow* • **75**

Example 17

If God Withdraweth, All the Cost

Johann Sebastian Bach

O Lord! How Many Miseries

Johann Sebastian Bach

Example 18. *O Lord! How Many Miseries* • 77

My Cause Is God's, and I Am Still

Johann Sebastian Bach

O Thou, of God the Father

Johann Sebastian Bach

Example 20. *O Thou, of God the Father* • **79**

Blessed Jesu, at Thy Word

Johann Sebastian Bach

Examples 22–23
TWO-PART INVENTIONS

Invention No. 4
Invention No. 8
Johann Sebastian Bach (1658–1750)

Terms and Concepts

In your own words, define the following *Terms and Concepts*. When necessary, refer to the *Glossary* at the back of the book.

Cadence

Canon

Counterpoint

Harmonic sequence

Imitation

Interval contraction

Interval expansion

Invention

Inversion, melodic

Melodic sequence

Modulation

Motive

Pedal point

Seventh chord

Texture

Triad

Study Questions

1. Listen to performances of *Examples 22* and *23* and identify the compositional devices in each piece.

2. Identify the key in which each invention begins and ends. (See *Information Bank, Topic 3.*) What type of minor scale(s) is used at the outset and conclusion of *Example 22*?

3. What factors supply unity and variety to each invention? (See *Information Bank, Topic 1.*)

4. How do the different tonalities in *Examples 22* and *23* help to divide each invention into sections? What other factors contribute to the sectionalization of each composition?

5. In *Example 22*, an octave leap in the lower part coupled with an anticipation and break in the rhythmic flow in the upper part are unique events that precede the final sonority of a cadence. Locate these events, and discuss their structural functions. Why is the restricted use of these events important to the listener?

6. In a Bach invention, the important motives are presented at the outset of the composition. Which motives are stated at the beginning of *Example 22*? Trace their use throughout the composition, and describe how they are manipulated and varied. Follow the same procedure for *Example 23*.

7. Compare *Example 22* with *Examples 8, 9,* and *46.* Among the points to compare are:

   (a) The texture
   (b) The degree of melodic similarity between the parts
   (c) The melodic and contrapuntal devices used
   (d) The tonal organization
   (e) The metric organization
   (f) The cadential procedures

8. In measures 21–23 of *Example 23,* a harmonic sequence is used. Consider root relationships, chord sonorities, and bass line. Does the sequential pattern continue in the following few measures? After the harmonic sequence, where is the key center established? What is the key?

Additional Activities

1. In a style of your choice, write and perform a two-part imitative composition. (In addition to the manuscript paper that follows, if necessary, use the manuscript paper provided at the back of the book.)

2. Write a single melody. Create a contrapuntal texture by having two or more instruments play the melody imitatively at different time intervals (for example, one measure apart, two beats apart, two measures apart).

3. Study other two-part inventions in *BURK* and *AAM.*

• Examples 22–23. Two-Part Inventions: J. S. Bach

Invention No. 4

Johann Sebastian Bach

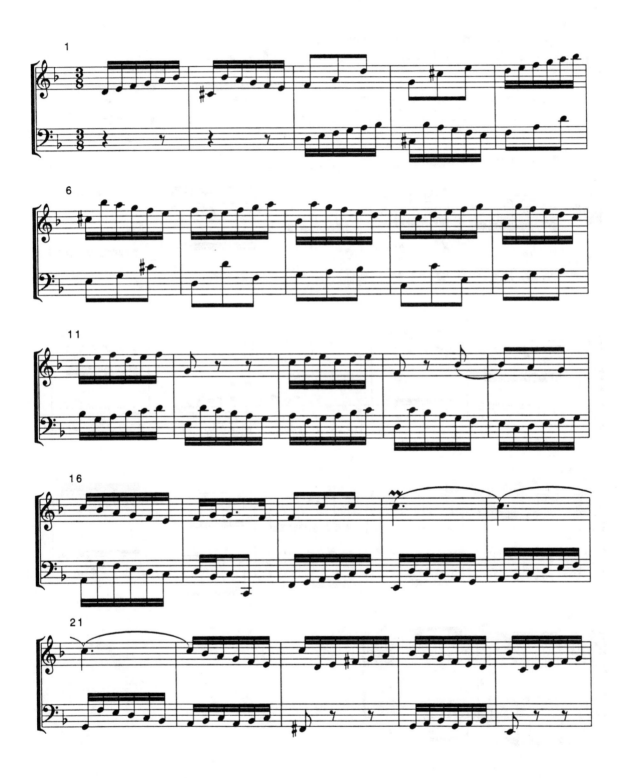

Example 22. *Invention No. 4* • **87**

Invention No. 8

Johann Sebastian Bach

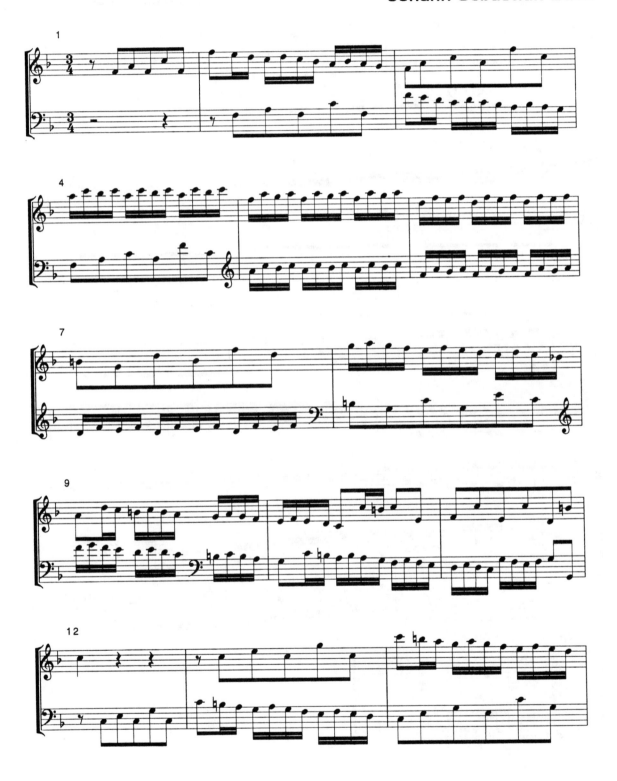

Example 23. *Invention No. 8* • **89**

90 • Examples 22–23. Two-Part Inventions: J. S. Bach

Example 24

THE WELL-TEMPERED
CLAVIER, BOOK I
Prelude and Fugue No. 16

Johann Sebastian Bach
(1685–1750)

Terms and Concepts

In your own words, define the following *Terms and Concepts*. When necessary, refer to the *Glossary* at the back of the book.

Answer

Cadence

Counterpoint

Counterpoint, invertible

Countersubject

Episode

Exposition

Fugue

Harmonic sequence

Imitation

Melodic sequence

Modulation

Motive

Pedal point

Prelude

Stretto

Subject

Tonal center

Study Questions

1. Identify the overall tonality of the prelude and that of the fugue. (See *Information Bank, Topic 3.*)

2. Both the prelude and the fugue have the meter C $\left(\frac{4}{4}\right)$. Should they be performed at the same tempo? (See *Information Bank, Topic 6.*)

3. The subject of the fugue is stated in measures 1 and 2. Trace the use of the subject throughout the composition. Discuss its motivic structure. Locate the use of these motives in the nonsubject material.

4. *Answer, countersubject, episode, exposition,* and *stretto* are terms commonly associated with the fugue. Discuss each in the context of *Example 24.*

5. To which keys does the fugue modulate? Compare the relation of these to the tonic key. Which same-key relationships are found in *Example 22?*

6. Identify the motives in the prelude, and trace their manipulation throughout.

7. In measures 9 and 10 of the prelude, a harmonic sequence is used. What is the relationship of the successive chord roots? Compare this harmonic sequence to the one in *Example 23* (refer to *Study Question 8* for *Examples 22–23*).

8. Compare this fugue to the one in *Example 54*. What identical procedures and devices are used?

9. Discuss how intensity is increased and dissipated in the prelude and in the fugue. (See *Information Bank, Topic 8*.)

Additional Activities

1. Listen to and study other preludes and fugues from Bach's *Well-Tempered Clavier* in *AAM* and *BURK*. Which identical procedures and devices do you discern aurally? visually?

The Well-Tempered Clavier, Book I
Prelude and Fugue No. 16

Johann Sebastian Bach

96 • Example 24. *The Well-Tempered Clavier*, Book I, J. S. Bach

98 • Example 24. *The Well-Tempered Clavier*, Book I, J. S. Bach

• Example 24. *The Well-Tempered Clavier*, Book I, J. S. Bach

Example 25
MINUET AND TRIO

Franz Joseph Haydn
(1732–1809)

Terms and Concepts

In your own words, define the following *Terms and Concepts*. When necessary, refer to the *Glossary* at the back of the book.

Binary form

Cadence

Contour

D. C. al fine

Fragmentation

Harmonic rhythm

Harmonic sequence

Inversion, harmonic

Melodic sequence

Minuet

Modulation

Motive

Nonchord tone

Pedal point

Period

Phrase

Rounded binary form

Seventh chord

Ternary form

Tonal center

Triad

Study Questions

1. Compare the stylistic features of these melodies to those in *Examples 1–5, 8–9, 15–16, 35, 46, 58*, and *60*. (See *Information Bank, Topic 2*.) What similarities do you find? How have melodic concepts changed throughout history?

2. What is the prevailing tonality of the minuet? of the trio? (See *Information Bank, Topic 3*.)

3. What structural term could be applied to measures 25–28 of the trio? to measures 25–32?

4. What is the form of the minuet? of the trio? of the minuet *and* trio? (See *Information Bank, Topics 4–5*.)

5. Assuming that at the outset of the minuet, the melodic motive in the right hand contains seven notes, what term describes the relationship of the second statement of this motive to the first? Where, in the ensuing measures, could the term *fragmentation* be applied?

6. In measures 1–10 of the minuet, Haydn provides various means for giving direction, momentum, intensity, and acceleration toward the cadence. Three of these means are harmonic rhythm, motive fragmentation, and contour. Discuss how each aids in this process. (See *Information Bank, Topics 7–8*.)

7. Do modulations occur in the minuet? in the trio? If so, in what measures(s) and to what key(s)?

8. Analyze the chords in measures 9–12 of the minuet. Could these measures be analyzed in one key and/or as a harmonic sequence?

9. What term could be applied to the bass pitch *small g* (see the *HDM* article "Pitch Names") of measures 33–40 of the trio? In which chords is it a chord member? In which chords is it not? Note the use of this device in the prelude of *Example 24*, measures 1–3 and measures 18–19.

10. Study the material found in measures 9–16 of the minuet. How does it compare to the material that precedes it and to the material that follows it? Follow this same procedure with the material presented in measures 33–40 of the trio.

Additional Activities

1. Compose a period structure that uses the following specifications:

   (a) The key of F major
   (b) Two parallel and symmetrical phrases
   (c) The range f^1 to f^2

   (In addition to the manuscript paper that follows, if necessary, use the manuscript paper provided at the back of the book.)

2. Compose another period that uses the following:

   (a) The key of G minor
   (b) Two contrasting and symmetrical (or asymmetrical) phrases
   (c) The range d^1 to a^2

3. Write a composition in ternary form using period structures in each section. Write the A section in a major key and the B section in the dominant of your chosen key.

Minuet and Trio

Franz Joseph Haydn

TRIO 25

D.C. al Fine

108 • Example 25. *Minuet and Trio,* Haydn

Example 26
LARGHETTO

Wolfgang Amadeus Mozart
(1756–91)

Terms and Concepts

In your own words, define the following *Terms and Concepts*. When necessary, refer to the *Glossary* at the back of the book.

Binary form

Cadence

Coda

Inversion, harmonic

Motive

Nonchord tone

Period

Phrase

Rounded binary form

Secondary chord

Seventh chord

Ternary form

Tonal center

Triad

Study Questions

1. What is the prevailing key of this composition? (See *Information Bank, Topic 3.*)

2. Assuming that measures 1–4 constitute a *phrase*, could this term be applied to measures 5–8? What structural term could be applied to measures 1–8?

3. What is the form of the entire composition? (See *Information Bank, Topics 4–5*.)

4. Provide a harmonic analysis for the composition and identify the nonchord tones.

5. Locate the deceptive cadence. Compare its location to that of the one in measures 48–49 of *Example 22*. What is the purpose of this cadence in each composition?

6. What structural term applies to measures 25–28?

7. Compare the final cadence of this composition to that of *Example 22*. What similarities and what differences are found?

Additional Activities

1. In a style of your choice, write a composition that exhibits the same structural design as *Example 26*. (In addition to the manuscript paper that follows, if necessary, use the manuscript paper provided at the back of the book.)

2. Compose a period structure that uses the following specifications:

   (a) The key of G major
   (b) Two parallel and symmetrical phrases
   (c) The range d^1 to g^2

3. Compose another period that uses the following:

   (a) The key of D minor
   (b) Two contrasting and symmetrical (or asymmetrical) phrases
   (c) The range d^1 to a^2

Larghetto

Wolfgang Amadeus Mozart

Example 27
ALLEGRO

Wolfgang Amadeus Mozart
(1756–91)

Terms and Concepts

In your own words, define the following *Terms and Concepts*. When necessary, refer to the *Glossary* at the back of the book.

Cadence

Interval contraction

Interval expansion

Inversion, melodic

Motive

Period

Phrase

Phrase extension

Tonal center

Study Questions

1. What is the prevailing key of this composition? (See *Information Bank, Topic 3.*)

2. Assuming that measures 1–6 constitute a *phrase*, is the term *phrase extension* applicable to this phrase? If so, where and how is the phrase extended? Is phrase extension used elsewhere in this composition?

3. Locate all of the phrases of this composition and identify those that are repeated. Are any of the phrases six measures in length?

4. Identify the melodic/rhythmic motives in both hands of the composition. (See *Information Bank, Topic 2*.) How is the right-hand motive that is stated at the outset (the seven eighth notes) manipulated to supply both unity and variety?

5. What structural term applies to the final two measures? Is this new or derivative material?

6. What type of cadence is used in measure 40? Compare this cadence to that found in measure 24 of *Example 26*. What musical purpose does each serve?

Additional Activities

1. Compose a period structure that uses the following specifications:

   (a) The key of C major
   (b) Two parallel and symmetrical phrases
   (c) The range c^1 to c^2

   (In addition to the manuscript paper that follows, if necessary, use the manuscript paper provided at the back of the book.)

Example 27

Allegro

Wolfgang Amadeus Mozart

Example 28
SONATINA
First Movement (Allegro)

Franz Joseph Haydn
(1732–1809)

Terms and Concepts

In your own words, define the following *Terms and Concepts*. When necessary, refer to the *Glossary* at the back of the book.

Change of mode

Exposition

Modulation

Rounded binary form

Sonata form

Sonatina

Tonal center

Study Questions

1. What is the prevailing tonality of this composition? (See *Information Bank, Topic 3.*) To which keys does the composition modulate?

2. This composition is an early example of sonata form. How does its overall structure resemble rounded binary form? See the minuet in *Example 25*.

3. Locate the exposition, development, and recapitulation in the composition. Locate the principal and subordinate sections within the exposition and within the recapitulation.

4. What musical features serve to contrast the principal and subordinate sections of the exposition? Compare the recapitulation with the exposition. Is the principle of contrast as pronounced in the recapitulation? Explain.

5. Distinguish between the terms *modulation* and *change of mode*. Where is each used in the composition?

Sonatina
First Movement (Allegro)

Franz Joseph Haydn

124 • Example 28. *Sonatina,* Haydn

Example 29

VARIATIONS ON A
SWISS SONG

Ludwig van Beethoven
(1770–1827)

Terms and Concepts

In your own words, define the following *Terms and Concepts*. When necessary, refer to the *Glossary* at the back of the book.

Articulation

Binary form

Change of mode

Dissonance

Dynamics

Form

Harmony

Melody

Meter

Modulation

Motive

Nonchord tone

Period

Phrase

Rhythm

Rounded binary form

Texture

Variation forms

Study Questions

1. In a theme and variations, each variation retains some aspects of the theme and varies others. Using the following list as a guide, analyze the theme of the composition to determine its individual characteristics:

(a) Melody and its melodic/rhythmic motives

(b) Bass pitches

(c) Harmony

(d) Phrases

(e) Overall form

(f) Overall key and, if used, modulation and change of mode

(g) Meter

(h) Tempo

(i) Articulation

(j) Instrumentation

(k) Texture

(l) Dynamics

(m) Degree of rhythmic activity

(n) Amount and types of dissonance

(o) Dramatic intensity

2. Compare each variation to the theme. Determine which aspects of the theme were retained and which were varied or abandoned. For example, circle the melody and bass pitches used in the theme and trace their presence in the corresponding measures of each variation.

3. Besides retaining certain aspects of the theme, each variation will exhibit individual features that serve to differentiate it from the theme and from other variations. Which features give each variation individuality? Consider the list in Question 1.

4. Examine the theme and variations as a single unified composition. Is there an increase in rhythmic activity, in textural complexity, and in the use of nonchord tones with each succeeding variation? (See *Information Bank, Topic 8.*) What other general observations can be made about the overall formal structure of this composition?

5. Compare the techniques of variation used in *Example 13* and *Example 58* with those used in *Example 29.*

Additional Activities

1. Using measures 1–8 of the trio in *Example 25* as a theme, write two or more variations. (In addition to the manuscript paper that follows, if necessary, use the manuscript paper provided at the back of the book.)

2. Write two or more variations on a theme of your choice (original or borrowed).

Variations on a Swiss Song

Ludwig van Beethoven

• Example 29. *Variations on a Swiss Song*, Beethoven

134 • Example 29. *Variations on a Swiss Song*, Beethoven

Example 30
RONDO

Wolfgang Amadeus Mozart
(1756–91)

Terms and Concepts

In your own words, define the following *Terms and Concepts*. When necessary, refer to the *Glossary* at the back of the book.

Double period

Form

Harmonic sequence

Period

Phrase

Rondo form

Ternary form

Tonal center

Study Questions

1. The form of this composition, expressed in letters, is **ABACA**. Locate the five sections. (See *Information Bank, Topic 5.*) Which features distinguish the contrasting sections? Compare the form of this composition with that of *Example 40*.

2. What structural term could be applied to measures 1–16? to measures 1–8? to measures 9–16? Is it possible to subdivide measures 1–8 and 9–16?

3. What is the prevailing key of each of the five sections? (See *Information Bank, Topic 3.*)

4. Locate and discuss the harmonic sequences used in the B and C sections. What is the relationship of the successive chord roots?

Additional Activities

1. Write a short composition in **ABACA** form. (In addition to the manuscript paper that follows, if necessary, use the manuscript paper provided at the back of the book.)

2. Locate and discuss other compositions that exhibit the rondo principle. Consider all styles of music. Consult the index of both *BURK* and *AAM*.

Rondo

Wolfgang Amadeus Mozart

140 • Example 30. *Rondo*, Mozart

Example 31
SONATA
Hob. XVI, No. 27
First Movement

Franz Joseph Haydn
(1732–1809)

Terms and Concepts

In your own words, define the following *Terms and Concepts*. When necessary, refer to the *Glossary* at the back of the book.

Alberti bass

Augmented sixth chord

Cadence

Cadential extension

Coda

Exposition

Harmonic sequence

Inversion, harmonic

Modulation

Murky bass

Nonchord tone

Rounded binary form

Secondary chord

Seventh chord

Sonata

Sonata form

Triad

Study Questions

1. After studying the principles of sonata form in *Example 28*, locate the exposition, development, and recapitulation in *Example 31*. Locate the principal, subordinate, and closing sections within the exposition and within the recapitulation.

2. Which features serve to contrast the principal and subordinate sections of the exposition? (See *Information Bank, Topics 1–2*.) Compare the recapitulation with the exposition. Is the principle of contrast as pronounced in the recapitulation? Explain.

3. Locate the use of Alberti bass and murky bass. What function do they serve in this sonata movement?

4. The last three measures of both the exposition and the recapitulation make up a cadential extension that provides tonal stability. What structural term could be applied to these measures?

5. Provide a harmonic analysis of the development. Locate each harmonic sequence and discuss how it is organized; for example, consider root relationships, chord sonorities, and bass lines.

6. Find the augmented sixth chords in the development. Identify the specific type of each augmented sixth chord.

7. Compare the content, structure, and scope of this composition with those of *Example 28*. What similarities do you find? What are the differences?

8. Which section of this composition exhibits the greatest intensity? (See *Information Bank, Topic 8.*) Discuss.

Additional Activities

1. The first movement of most symphonies, string quartets, and piano sonatas by Haydn, Mozart, and Beethoven is in sonata form. Listen to, discuss, and, if possible, perform other movements that are in sonata form.

Sonata, Hob. XVI, No. 27
First Movement

Franz Joseph Haydn

146 • Example 31. *Sonata*, Hob. XVI, No. 27, Haydn

• Example 31. *Sonata*, Hob. XVI, No. 27, Haydn

Example 32
SONATA
K. 333

Wolfgang Amadeus Mozart
(1756–91)

Terms and Concepts

In your own words, define the following *Terms and Concepts*. When necessary, refer to the *Glossary* at the back of the book. Begin by reviewing the *Terms and Concepts* for *Examples 28, 30,* and *31.*

Articulation

Compositional devices

Double period

Dynamics

Melodic sequence

Melody

Meter

Motive

Rhythm

Texture

Study Questions

General Questions

1. Review *Examples 28, 30,* and *31.*

2. Contrast, an important feature of Classical style, can be seen both in a single movement (internally) and between the movements of a multimovement composition (externally). (See *Information Bank, Topics 1* and *7–8.*) How does each of the following concepts provide contrast between the movements?

(a) Overall key
(b) Tempo
(c) Meter
(d) Thematic material
(e) Performance instructions
(f) Affection
(g) Relative degree of intensity

3. As stated in Question 2, contrast in Classical style is often applied internally. How does each of the following concepts provide contrast within each movement?

   (a) Overall form
   (b) Modulation
   (c) Change of mode
   (d) Dynamics
   (e) Amount and degree of melodic contrast
   (f) Articulation
   (g) Degree of rhythmic activity
   (h) Contrast of affections

4. Unity is also an important feature in Classical style, both within a single movement and between the various movements of a multimovement composition. How is unity achieved in this sonata, both internally and externally? Consider the lists given in the two preceding questions as topics for discussion.

5. Using this composition as an example of Classical style, compare the degree of contrast found here with that found in Baroque compositions (for instance, see *Examples 22–24*). Using the list given in Question 3, identify the factors that supply both unity and contrast in Baroque compositions.

6. A *transition*, a section of music that links contrasting or similar thematic sections, may also fulfill one or more of the following concomitant functions:

   (a) Modulation
   (b) Development of previously used material
   (c) Introduction of new material
   (d) Introduction of melodic/rhythmic material that foreshadows upcoming material
   (e) Preparation of the listener for a change of affection

   Measures 11–22 in the exposition of the first movement could be considered a transition between the principal and subordinate sections. Which of the preceding functions does this transition fulfill? Locate other transitions in each movement and describe their functions.

7. Diagram the formal structure of each movement. Use letters to identify thematic material. Give the measures and key(s) for each section. (See *Information Bank, Topics 3–5.*)

8. If the general tempo of each movement were not given, how could you determine it? (See *Information Bank, Topic 6.*)

Questions on the First Movement

9. What is the form of measures 1–10? Is phrase extension used? Explain.

10. Locate and identify the types of cadences in measures 23–38 (up to the second beat). What is the prevailing tonality of this section? (See *Information Bank, Topic 3.*) What structural term best describes this section?

11. What type of nonchord tone is used on the first count of each of the first five measures? To what extent is this nonchord tone used throughout the movement? (See also *Study Question 4* for *Example 36.*)

12. How does the transition between the principal and subordinate sections of the exposition vary with the corresponding transition in the recapitulation? How are they similar? (*See* Question 6.)

13. What melodic/harmonic device is used in measures 47–48?

14. Does the exposition contain a coda? What is the structural significance of the trill in measure 58? (*See* Question 26.)

15. In sonata-form movements of the Classical period, the development (rather that the exposition or the recapitulation) is often the section of the movement with the greatest contrast, intensity, and instability. These qualities can be achieved by one or more of the following:

(a) Modulation
(b) Change of mode
(c) Sequence (melodic and/or harmonic)
(d) Motive development
(e) Thematic variation
(f) New motives and/or themes
(g) Change in dynamics
(h) Change in rhythmic activity

(i) Change in texture

(j) Change in orchestration

Using this list, analyze the development to determine how contrast, intensity, and instability are achieved.

16. Identify the harmony on the fourth beat of measure 80. How does the placement and function of this chord compare with the chord found in measure 84 of *Example 31*.

17. Compare the structure, content, and scope of this movement with those of *Example 28*. What similarities do you find? What are the differences?

Questions on the Second Movement

18. What structural term applies to measures 1–8? to measures 14–21? to measures 22–29? to measures 29–31?

19. What is the derivation of the melodic material used in the development of the second movement? Does the development contain any melodic/rhythmic material not used in the exposition?

20. How are contrast, intensity, and instability achieved in this movement? (*See* Question 15.)

21. Identify the chord on the first beat of measure 3. Does it function as a secondary leading-tone chord? Explain.

22. What type of cadence concludes measures 1–8?

23. Compare measures 1–8 with measures 51–58. How does the material presented in measures 51–58 supply both unity and variety? Locate other examples in the recapitulation that also vary with the corresponding presentation in the exposition.

Questions on the Third Movement

24. Compare the form of this movement with the form of *Examples 30* and *40*. (See *Information Bank, Topic 5*.) What formal principles characterize the rondo? (*See* Question 3.) Consider both the thematic and harmonic design.

25. What structural term applies to measures 1–16? to measures 1–8? to measures 9–16? to measures 1–4?

26. What common purpose do the trills serve in measures 37 and 58 of the first movement? Compare the trill in measure 58 of the first movement with that in measure 212 of this third movement. What structural section does the trill precede in both instances?

Sonata, K. 333

Wolfgang Amadeus Mozart

I

158 • Example 32. *Sonata*, K. 333, Mozart

160 • Example 32. *Sonata*, K. 333, Mozart

162 • Example 32. *Sonata*, K. 333, Mozart

II

Andante cantabile

164 • Example 32. *Sonata*, K. 333, Mozart

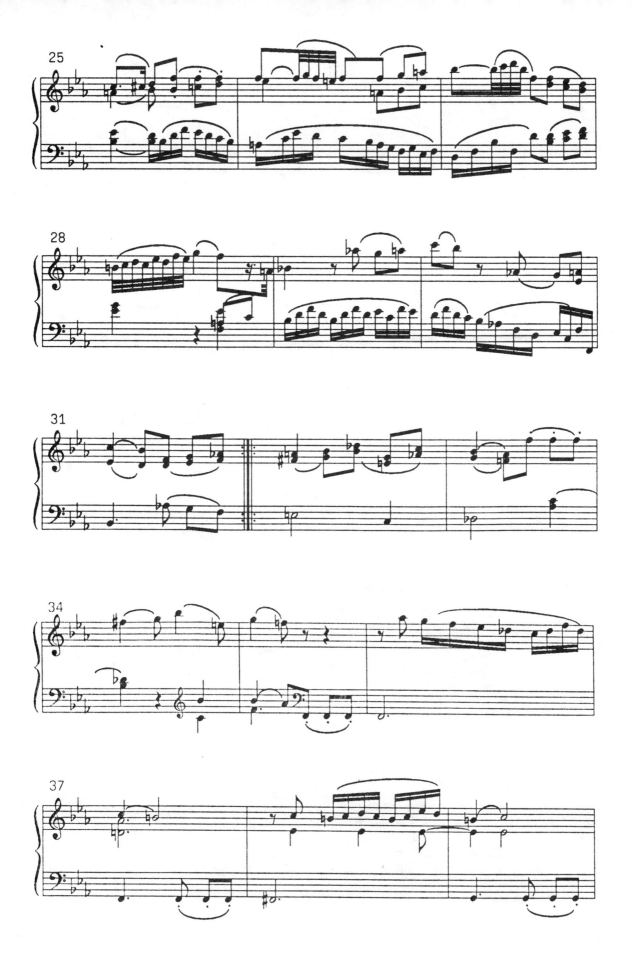

• Example 32. *Sonata*, K. 333, Mozart

III

Allegretto grazioso.

170 • Example 32. *Sonata,* K. 333, Mozart

172 • Example 32. *Sonata*, K. 333, Mozart

174 • Example 32. *Sonata*, K. 333, Mozart

176 • Example 32. *Sonata*, K. 333, Mozart

178 • Example 32. *Sonata*, K. 333, Mozart

Example 33
WALTZ

Franz Schubert
(1797–1828)

Terms and Concepts

In your own words, define the following *Terms and Concepts*. When necessary, refer to the *Glossary* at the back of the book.

Accent

Augmented sixth chord

Binary form

Character piece

179

Contour

Double period

Harmonic rhythm

Inversion, harmonic

Metric accent

Neapolitan sixth chord

Period

Phrase

Rounded binary form

Secondary chord

Seventh chord

Ternary form

Triad

Waltz

Study Questions

1. Assuming that measures 1–4 constitute a *phrase*, what structural term applies to measures 1–8? to measures 9–16? to measures 1–16?

2. What formal structure best describes the entire composition? (See *Information Bank, Topics 4–5.*)

3. Assuming the key of the composition is A minor throughout, provide a harmonic analysis. Identify the secondary dominant and secondary leading-tone chords, the Neapolitan sixth chord, and the augmented sixth chords.

4. Compare the Neapolitan sixth chord of this composition with that of *Example 35*, measure 12. What similarities and differences are present?

5. In measures 1–8, how is the drive to the cadence achieved? (See *Information Bank, Topic 8.*) In answering this, consider harmony, harmonic rhythm, melodic contour, and rhythmic activity.

6. Analyze the basic pitch structure of the melody in measures 25–32 by identifying the pitches that are emphasized. How does this melodic skeleton help release tension and thereby bring the composition to a convincing conclusion? What other factors aid in this process?

Additional Activities

1. Using the harmony of measures 1–8, compose a period structure based on a motive of your choice. (In addition to the manuscript paper that follows, if necessary, use the manuscript paper provided at the back of the book.)

2. Compose an eight-measure period using the following chord progression:

   Phrase 1: I, VI, IV, V
   Phrase 2: I, IV, N6–V, I

Waltz

Franz Schubert

Example 34

DIE WINTERREISE

Op. 89

"Muth"

Franz Schubert

(1797–1828)

Terms and Concepts

In your own words, define the following *Terms and Concepts*. When necessary, refer to the *Glossary* at the back of the book.

Bar form

Binary form

Change of mode

Lied

Modulation

Ternary form

Text painting

Study Questions

1. Define all performance instructions.

2. Which of the following best describes the form of this lied: bar, binary, or ternary? In answering this, consider the text, tonal organization, vocal line, and opening and closing piano sections.

3. How do the vocal and piano parts help to reflect and interpret the text? Is the piano part merely an accompaniment, or is this composition a duet for voice and piano? Discuss the piano's various roles.

4. Locate the modulations and change of mode. Speculate why the key of A minor is used in measures 31–32.

Additional Activities

1. Compose a song in either bar, binary, or ternary form using harmonic and melodic styles of your choice. You may also wish to write your own text. (In addition to the manuscript paper that follows, if necessary, use the manuscript paper provided at the back of the book.)

2. Analyze other lieder found in *BURK* and *AAM*.

• Example 34. *Die Winterreise,* Op. 89, "Muth," Schubert

Die Winterreise, Op 89
"Muth"

Franz Schubert

Translation

Courage

Blows the snow in my face, I brush it away,
When my heart cries loudly, I sing loudly and gaily.

I won't hear what it tells me, I have stopped my ears,
Will not understand its cries, crying is for fools.

Merrily I meet the world, braving wind and weather!
If there is no God on earth, we are gods ourselves!

190 • Example 34. *Die Winterreise,* Op. 89, "Muth," Schubert

Wet- ter! will kein Gott auf Er- den sein,

Sind wir sel- ber Got-ter.

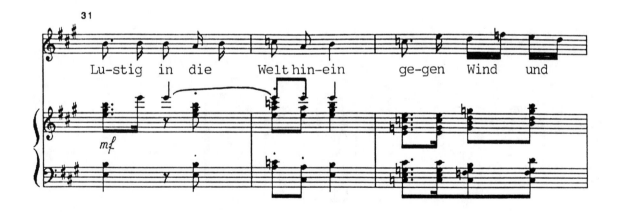

Lu-stig in die Welt hin-ein ge-gen Wind und

Example 35
ALBUM LEAVES
Op. 124
Waltz

Robert Schumann
(1810-56)

Terms and Concepts

In your own words, define the following *Terms and Concepts*. When necessary, refer to the *Glossary* at the back of the book.

Articulation

Augmented sixth chord

Binary form

Character piece

Contour

Double period

Dynamics

Form

Harmonic sequence

Interval

Inversion, harmonic

Melody

Meter

Modulation

Neapolitan sixth chord

Nonchord tone

Period

Phrase

Range

Rhythm

Rounded binary form

Secondary chord

Seventh chord

Tempo

Ternary form

Tessitura

Texture

Tonal center

Triad

Study Questions

1. Compare the stylistic features of this melody with those in *Examples 1–5, 8–9, 15–16, 25, 46, 58,* and *60.* (See *Information Bank, Topic 2.*) What similarities do you find? How have melodic concepts changed throughout history?

2. Assuming that the first two periods are each eight measures long, how many phrases does each period contain? What term best describes the relationship between the two periods? Could measures 1–16 also be analyzed as a single period? Explain.

3. Review the form of *Example 25*. What is the form of *Example 35*? (See *Information Bank, Topic 4*.)

4. Assuming that measures 1–16 are in the key of A minor, provide a harmonic analysis.

5. With what type of chord does the composition begin? What is its harmonic function?

6. Identify the chord in measure 12. Discuss its structural placement and resolution. How is it used similarly in *Example 33*, measures 21–22?

7. Beginning at the double bar and using the pitches in the left hand as a guide, provide a harmonic analysis in the key of F major for measures 17–28. What types of dissonance are used in the right hand?

8. What melodic device is used in the right hand in measures 21–28? Could these measures be viewed as a harmonic sequence? Explain. What is the relationship between successive chord roots in this section?

Additional Activities

1. In a style of your choice, write a composition that exhibits ternary form. (In addition to the manuscript paper that follows, if necessary, use the manuscript paper provided at the back of the book.)

2. Compose a period structure that uses the following specifications:
   (a) The key of C major
   (b) Two parallel and symmetrical phrases
   (c) The range of c^1 to e^2

3. Compose another period that uses the following:
   (a) The key of B Minor
   (b) Two contrasting and symmetrical (or asymmetrical) phrases
   (c) The range *small* b^1 to d^2

4. Write a composition in ternary form using period structures in each section. Write the A-section in a major key and the B-section in the dominant of your chosen key.

• Example 35. *Album Leaves,* Op. 124, R. Schumann

Album Leaves, Op. 124
Waltz

Robert Schumann

Example 36
IMPROMPTU
Op. 5, No. 5

Robert Schumann
(1810–56)

Terms and Concepts

In your own words, define the following *Terms and Concepts*. When necessary, refer to the *Glossary* at the back of the book.

Binary form

Character piece

Inversion, harmonic

Modulation

Motive

Nonchord tone

Period

Phrase

Rounded binary form

Seventh chord

Ternary form

Triad

Study Questions

1. What structural term could be applied to measures 1–4? to measures 1–8? Are the same structures also present in measures 9–16?

2. Is this composition in binary, rounded binary, or ternary form? Explain.

3. Provide a harmonic analysis. Does a modulation occur? If so, where, what type, and to what key?

4. Which nonchord tones are used on the first beat of each of the first six measures? To what extent are these nonchord tones used throughout the composition? Review *Study Question 11* for *Example 32*.

5. Identify and trace each melodic/rhythmic motive used throughout the composition. (See *Information Bank, Topic 1*.) How does each motive provide both unity and variety?

Additional Activities

1. For an instrument of your choice, write a one-period composition that contains two phrases. (In addition to the manuscript paper that follows, if necessary, use the manuscript paper provided at the back of the book.)

2. Compose a melodic/rhythmic motive. Expand this motive into a binary composition.

Impromptu, Op. 5, No. 5

Robert Schumann

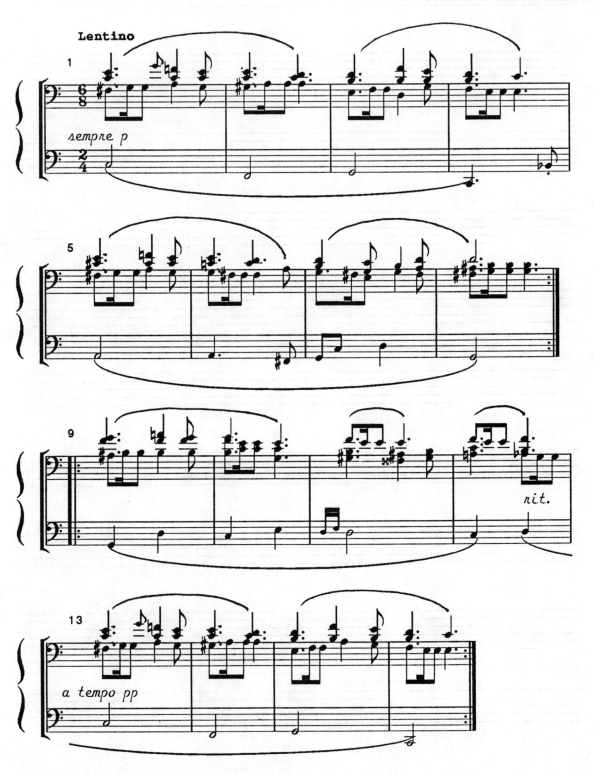

Example 37
DU BIST WIE EINE
BLUME
Op. 25, No. 24

Robert Schumann
(1810–56)

Terms and Concepts

In your own words, define the following *Terms and Concepts*. When necessary, refer to the *Glossary* at the back of the book.

Augmented sixth chord

Cadence

Coda

Double period

Inversion, harmonic

Lied

Period

Phrase

Prelude

Secondary chord

Seventh chord

Text painting

Triad

Study Questions

1. What factors help to sectionalize this lied? Consider the text, vocal line, piano part, and harmony.

2. What structural term applies to measures 1–9? to measures 10–17? to measures 1–17?

3. How does the piano part contribute to the interpretation of the text? Is it merely an accompaniment or is it an equal participant with the voice in projecting the meaning of the text?

4. What musical purpose is served by the final four measures? What structural term applies to these measures? Compare the role of these concluding measures with that of the final four measures of *Example 34*.

5. Assuming the composition remains in the key of F major, provide a harmonic analysis. Is it possible to modulate to C major in measures 7–9? Locate and identify the secondary dominant and secondary leading-tone chords. How is the secondary dominant in measure 15, beat 2 altered? Is this same alteration used elsewhere in the composition?

6. A German augmented sixth chord is used in measure 7. What is the root of this chord? Explain how the German (or Italian) augmented sixth chord functions as a secondary leading-tone chord; for example, vii7/II in F major (or, if a modulation to C is used, a vii7/V). Compare the function and resolution of the chord used in this example to that of the first chord in *Example 35*.

Du Bist Wie Eine Blume
Op. 25, No. 24

Robert Schumann

• Example 37. *Du Bist Wie Eine Blume*, Op. 25, No. 24, R. Schumann

Example 38

PRELUDE
Op. 28, No. 7

Frédéric Chopin
(1810–49)

Terms and Concepts

In your own words, define the following *Terms and Concepts*. When necessary, refer to the *Glossary* at the back of the book.

Character piece

Double period

Inversion, harmonic

Motive

Ninth chord

Nonchord tone

Period

Phrase

Prelude

Seventh chord

Triad

Study Questions

1. Identify the motive that is used throughout the composition. How is it modified?

2. What structural term could be applied to measures 1–8? to measures 9–16? to the entire composition?

3. Assuming this composition remains in one key, provide a harmonic analysis. Locate and identify the secondary chords.

4. How do the chords used by Chopin in measures 6 and 14 expand the harmonic language used in the eighteenth century? (See *Examples 13–32.*)

5. Locate and identify the nonchord tones. How does the consistent use of the dotted eighth note lend unity?

Additional Activities

1. Compose a phrase for piano that demonstrates the use of ninth chords. (In addition to the manuscript paper that follows, if necessary, use the manuscript paper provided at the back of the book.)

2. Listen to and analyze other Chopin preludes in *BURK* and *AAM*.

• Example 38. *Prelude,* Op. 28, No. 7, Chopin

Prelude, Op. 28, No. 7

Frédéric Chopin

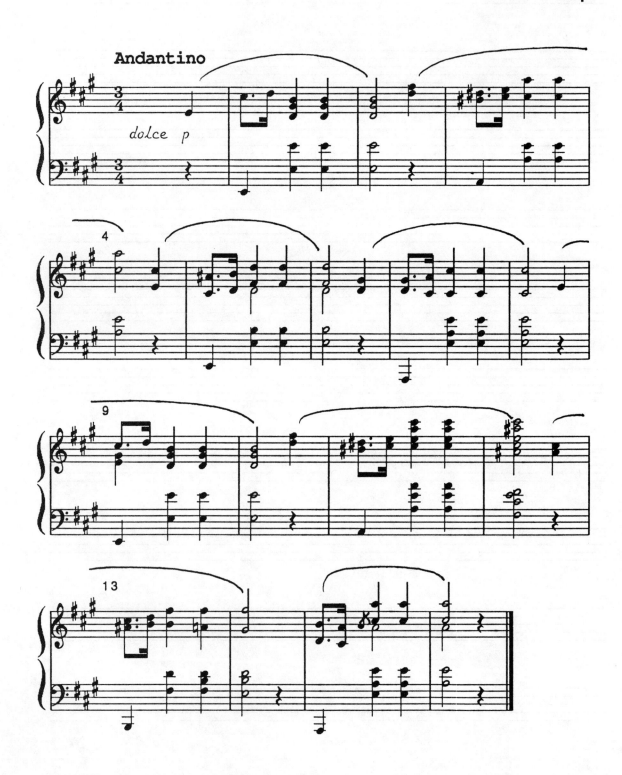

Example 39
PRELUDE
Op. 28, No. 20

Frédéric Chopin
(1810–49)

Terms and Concepts

In your own words, define the following *Terms and Concepts*. When necessary, refer to the *Glossary* at the back of the book.

Character piece

Double period

Harmonic sequence

Inversion, harmonic

Melodic sequence

Motive

Nonchord tone

Period

Phrase

Prelude

Secondary chord

Seventh chord

Triad

Study Questions

1. How many phrases does this composition contain? How are the phrases delineated? What structural term applies to this entire composition?

2. One motive is used throughout this composition. Identify this motive and its modifications. Is this same procedure used in *Examples 36* and *38*? Discuss.

3. Compare measure 1 with measure 2. What melodic and harmonic devices are used in these measures?

4. Provide a harmonic analysis of the entire composition. Locate and identify the non-chord tones.

Additional Activities

1. Compose a period for piano that demonstrates the use of harmonic and melodic sequences. (In addition to the manuscript paper that follows, if necessary, use the manuscript paper provided at the back of the book.)

2. Compose a short character piece that conveys a descriptive idea. Perform your composition to determine whether your descriptive idea is conveyed to others.

• Example 39. *Prelude,* Op. 28, No. 20, Chopin

Prelude, Op. 28, No. 20

Frédéric Chopin

Example 40
MAZURKA
Op. 7, No. 1

Frédéric Chopin
(1810–49)

Terms and Concepts

In your own words, define the following *Terms and Concepts*. When necessary, refer to the *Glossary* at the back of the book.

Character piece

Double period

Mazurka

Minuet

Ninth chord

Nonchord tone

Pedal point

Period

Phrase

Rondo form

Study Questions

1. Define all performance instructions.

2. Discuss the characteristics of the mazurka. Compare this dance with the minuet (see *Example 25*) and with the waltz (see *Examples 33* and *41*).

3. What is the form of the entire composition? (See *Information Bank, Topics 4–5.*) How does it compare with *Example 30*?

4. Discuss the structure of measures 1–24.

5. What device is used in measures 45–51 of the left hand? Is this device used elsewhere in the movement? If so, where? Locate the use of this device in *Example 45*.

6. Analyze the half note e' in measures 6 and 10. Is it a nonchord tone in each measure? Explain.

7. Analyze the chord in measure 5. Is this type of chord used in measure 1? Is it used elsewhere in the composition? Review *Study Question 4* for *Example 38*.

Additional Activities

1. Write or improvise a melody against a pedal point. (In addition to the manuscript paper that follows, if necessary, use the manuscript paper provided at the back of the book.)

2. Study other compositions by Chopin in *AAM* and *BURK*.

3. Write a short composition in **ABACA** form.

4. Locate and discuss other compositions that exhibit the rondo principle. Consider all styles of music. Consult the indexes of both *BURK* and *AAM*.

Mazurka, Op. 7, No. 1

Frédéric Chopin

232 • Example 40. *Mazurka*, Op. 7, No. 1, Chopin

Example 41
WALTZ
Op. 39, No. 15

Johannes Brahms
(1833–97)

Terms and Concepts

In your own words, define the following *Terms and Concepts*. When necessary, refer to the *Glossary* at the back of the book.

Binary form

Character piece

Coda

Double period

Harmonic sequence

Inversion, harmonic

Motive

Period

Phrase

Rounded binary form

Secondary chord

Seventh chord

Ternary form

Triad

Waltz

Study Questions

1. Discuss the characteristics of the waltz (see also *Example 33*). Compare this dance with the minuet (see *Example 25*) and with the mazurka (see *Example 40*).

2. What is the form of *Example 41*? (See *Information Bank, Topics 4–5.*)

3. Identify the motive used throughout this composition. (See *Study Question 2* for *Example 39.*)

4. Is new motivic material used in measures 37–44? Explain. What structural term applies to this section?

5. Analyze and discuss the phrasing of measures 1–8. Compare measures 1–8 with measures 9–16 and with measures 23–30.

6. Provide a harmonic analysis of measures 1–16. The dominant chord in the key of A♭ major is not used in these measures. What effect does this have on the harmonic and structural organization?

7. Should measures 17–23 be analyzed harmonically in a key (A♭ major) or as a harmonic sequence? In answering this, consider root relationships, chord sonorities, and bass line.

Waltz, Op. 39, No. 15

Johannes Brahms

238 • Example 41. *Waltz*, Op. 39, No. 15, Brahms

Example 42
MORGEN

Richard Strauss
(1864–1949)

Terms and Concepts

In your own words, define the following *Terms and Concepts*. When necessary, refer to the *Glossary* at the back of the book.

Lied

Ninth chord

Nonchord tone

Prelude

Strophic

Text painting

Through-composed

Study Questions

Before answering these questions, review *Examples 34* and *37*.

1. Does *strophic* or *through-composed* best describe the form of this Strauss lied? Explain.

2. How do the vocal and piano parts help to reflect and interpret the text? Is the piano part merely an accompaniment or is this composition a duet for voice and piano?

3. What purposes are served by the solo piano sections? Compare their uses here with their uses in *Examples 34* and *37*.

4. Study the melodic material used in the piano prelude. Trace its use throughout the composition.

5. Analyze the chord in measures 31–32. Is the f^1 treated as a chord tone or as a nonchord tone? Explain.

Additional Activities

1. Select a poem that lends itself to musical text painting. Compose a melody for this poem that demonstrates text painting. (In addition to the manuscript paper that follows, if necessary, use the manuscript paper provided at the back of the book.)

2. Listen to several examples of contemporary vocal music. Do any exhibit text painting?

Morgen

Richard Strauss

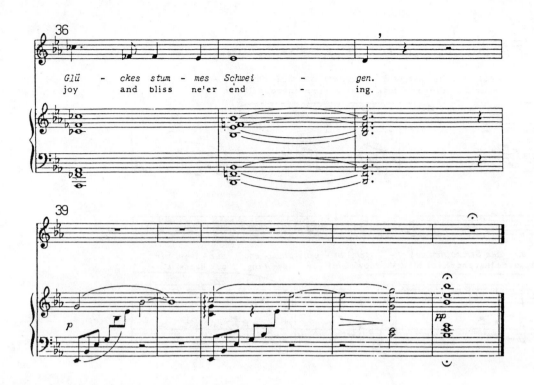

• Example 42. *Morgen*, R. Strauss

Example 43

PICTURES AT AN EXHIBITION

"Promenade"

Modest Mussorgsky

(1839–81)

Terms and Concepts

In your own words, define the following *Terms and Concepts*. When necessary, refer to the *Glossary* at the back of the book.

Concert pitch

Meter, mixed

Nonchord tone

Nontransposing instrument

Program music

Transposing instrument

Study Questions

1. Identify all the instruments listed on the score for *Example 43*.

2. Define all the performance instructions.

3. Distinguish between transposing and nontransposing instruments. Which instruments in this excerpt are transposing? Which sound an octave lower than written? Derive the concert pitches for each of the transposing instruments.

4. What musical effect is created by mixed meters? (See also *Example 64.*) Could Mussorgsky have used $\frac{11}{4}$ meter? a combination of $\frac{2}{4}$ and $\frac{3}{4}$ meters? Discuss.

5. "Promenade" is a musical representation of a person walking from one picture to another at an art exhibition. How is this programmatic suggestion conveyed by the music?

Additional Activities

1. Learn to distinguish orchestral instruments from one another by listening to classroom demonstrations and to recorded performances of compositions such as *Young Person's Guide to the Orchestra* by Benjamin Britten and *Peter and the Wolf* by Sergei Prokofiev.

2. Orchestrate a Bach chorale (see *Examples 15–21*) for available classroom instruments. Perform each orchestration. Orchestrate and perform other compositions. (In addition to the manuscript paper that follows, if necessary, use the manuscript paper provided at the back of the book.)

3. Listen to the entire *Pictures at an Exhibition*. Discuss the programmatic suggestions of each section and the structural role of "Promenade."

Pictures at an Exhibition
"Promenade"

Modest Mussorgsky

Example 44

POEME

Op. 69, No. 1

Alexander Scriabin

(1872-1915)

Terms and Concepts

In your own words, define the following *Terms and Concepts*. When necessary, refer to the *Glossary* at the back of the book.

Binary form

Character piece

Harmonic sequence

Harmony

Melodic sequence

Mystic chord

Phrase

Repetition

Study Questions

1. This composition is based primarily on the harmonic sonority commonly known as the *mystic chord*: C, F♯, B♭, E, A, and D. Identify the different types of fourths used to construct this sonority.

2. Trace the harmonic use of the mystic chord (and its transpositions) throughout the composition.

3. Using the pitches of the mystic chord, construct a scale beginning on the pitch C. Trace the melodic use of this scale (and its transpositions) throughout the composition.

4. What term best describes the relationship between measures 1–4 and measures 5–8? between measures 9–10 and measures 11–12? Locate other uses of these devices throughout the composition.

5. Compare measures 1–16 with measures 17–32 and measures 1–3 with measures 33–36. What term best describes the overall form of this composition? (See *Information Bank, Topics 4–5*.)

Additional Activities

1. Construct the mystic chord on the pitch F. Using the pitches of this chord, construct a scale beginning on F. Write a short composition using this chord and scale. Provide variety by transposing the chord and scale to different pitch levels. (In addition to the manuscript paper that follows, if necessary, use the manuscript paper provided at the back of the book.)

2. Construct your own chord (six to eight pitches), and write a short composition following the above procedures.

3. In *MTTM*, read and discuss Chapter 2, "Scale Formations in Twentieth-Century Music," and Chapter 3, "The Vertical Dimension: Chords and Simultaneities."

Poeme, Op. 69, No. 1

Alexander Scriabin

258 • Example 44. *Poeme*, Op. 69, No. 1, Scriabin

Example 45

PRELUDES

Book I

No 2, "Voiles" ("Sails")

Claude Achille Debussy

(1862–1918)

Terms and Concepts

In your own words, define the following *Terms and Concepts*. When necessary, refer to the *Glossary* at the back of the book.

Cadence

Character piece

Dissonance

Enharmonic

Impressionism

Meter

Motive

Nonchord tone

Pedal point

Pentatonic scale

Prelude

Tonal center

Whole-tone scale

Study Questions

1. Translate and define all the performance instructions used in this composition. How have performance instructions changed throughout music history? Compare these instructions with others in this anthology.

2. What scales are used to construct the melodic and harmonic materials in this composition? How do these scales help to define the overall form?

3. Locate the enharmonic pitches in this composition (for example, G♯ and A♭ in measure 15). Why are they used?

4. Does this composition use harmonic dissonance (passing tone, suspension, and so on)? If not, how is momentum and direction achieved? (See *Information Bank, Topic 8.*)

5. Identify the motives in this composition and trace their ensuing modifications. How do they help to provide both unity and variety? (See *Information Bank, Topics 1–2.*)

6. Locate the cadences in this composition. How does Debussy achieve cadential effects? Do they convey a particular tonal center? (See *Information Bank, Topic 3.*) Discuss.

7. Is the meter aurally discernible? Discuss the factors that define it and those that obscure it.

Additional Activities

1. Write and perform a composition in ternary form. Use the pentatonic scale in each A-section and the whole-tone scale in the B-section. (In addition to the manuscript paper that follows, if necessary, use the manuscript paper provided at the back of the book.)

2. Compare and discuss the relationship of the whole-tone scale to a scale based on the mystic chord (see *Study Question 2* for *Example 44*).

3. Study other compositions that use the whole-tone and pentatonic scales (consult the indexes of both *BURK* and *AAM*).

4. Read and discuss Chapter 2, "Scale Formations in Twentieth-Century Music," in *MTTM*.

Preludes, Book I
No. 2, "Voiles" ("Sails")

Claude Achille Debussy

264 • Example 45. *Preludes*, Book I, Debussy

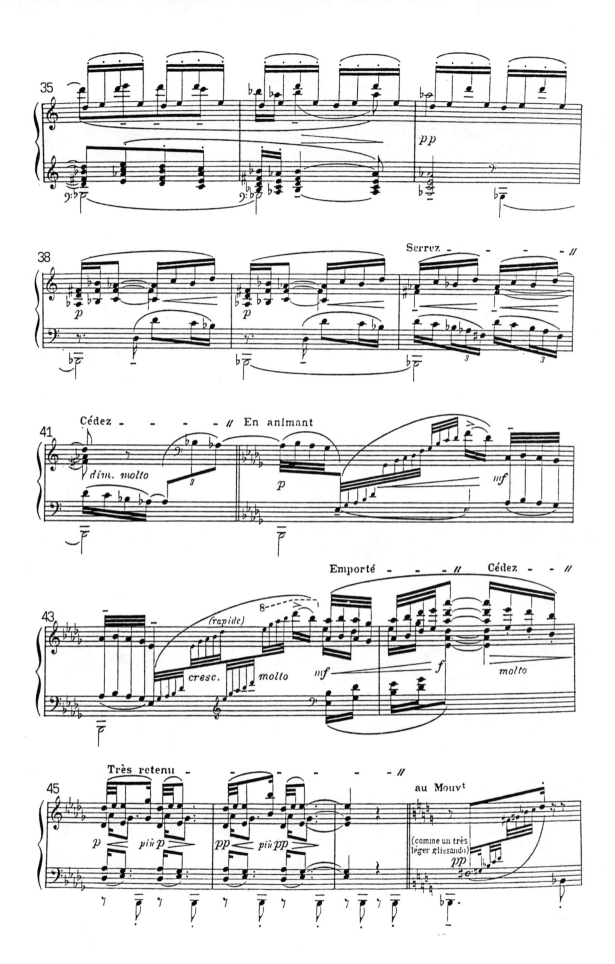

• Example 45. *Preludes*, Book I, Debussy

Examples 46–47
MIKROKOSMOS
No. 37, No. 59

Béla Bartók
(1881–1945)

Terms and Concepts

In your own words, define the following *Terms and Concepts*. When necessary, refer to the *Glossary* at the back of the book.

Accent

Bimodality

Binary form

Cadence

Canon

Contour

Counterpoint

Counterpoint, invertible

Dynamics

Fragmentation

Form

Imitation

Interval contraction

Interval expansion

Inversion, melodic

Melodic sequence

Melody

Meter

Modes, melodic

Motive

Period

Phrase

Range

Repetition

Rhythm

Stretto

Tempo

Ternary form

Tessitura

Texture

Tonal center

Study Questions

1. Compare the stylistic features of these melodies with those in *Examples 1–5, 8–9, 15–16, 25, 35, 58,* and *60.* (See *Information Bank, Topic 2.*) What similarities do you find? How have melodic concepts changed throughout history?

2. Which of the following are used in each of these compositions:

(a) Imitation

(b) Melodic sequence

(c) Canon

(d) Melodic inversion

(e) Invertible counterpoint

(f) Stretto

How do these devices provide unity to each composition? How do they provide variety? (See *Information Bank, Topic 1.*)

3. Identify the motives in each composition. Trace their use throughout each composition.

4. The use of two independent melodic lines characterizes each of these compositions. What contributes to this independence? Consider such factors as:

(a) Harmonic intervals

(b) Rhythmic organization

(c) Texture

(d) Melodic pitch materials

(e) Accents

Additional Activities

1. Using the forms, devices, and techniques found in Bartók's music (*Examples 46–49*), write and perform several short compositions. (In addition to the manuscript paper that follows, if necessary, use the manuscript paper provided at the back of the book.)

2. Study the examples of Bartók listed in the index of *MTTM*.

3. In a style of your choice, write and perform a two-part imitative composition.

4. Write a single melody. Create a contrapuntal texture by having two or more instruments play the melody imitatively at different time intervals (for example, one measure apart, two beats apart, two measures apart).

Mikrokosmos, No. 37

Béla Bartók

Example 46. *Mikrokosmos*, No. 37 • **273**

Mikrokosmos, No. 59

Béla Bartók

Example 48
MIKROKOSMOS
No. 78

Béla Bartók
(1881–1945)

Terms and Concepts

In your own words, define the following *Terms and Concepts*. When necessary, refer to the *Glossary* at the back of the book.

Accent

Binary form

Canon

Fragmentation

Imitation

Interval contraction

Interval expansion

Melodic sequence

Modes, melodic

Motive

Ostinato

Phrase

Repetition

Ternary form

Tonal center

Study Questions

1. Using the procedures suggested in *Study Questions* for *Examples 46–47*, analyze the melodic materials. What is the tonal center? Which melodic mode or scale is used? (See *Information Bank, Topic 3*.)

2. The first phrase is four measures long. Trace the use of this phrase and its motives throughout the composition. How is it developed? Consider the following concepts:

   (a) Repetition
   (b) Melodic sequence
   (c) Fragmentation
   (d) Motivic variation

3. A four-note ostinato is used in the right hand of measures 20–24. Where else is this device used in the composition? What is the origin of these four notes?

4. What is the form of this composition? (See *Information Bank, Topics 4–5.*) How is this form determined? In answering this, consider the pitch materials, phrasing, and accents.

Additional Activities

1. Compose an ostinato for a pitched or rhythm instrument. Compose or improvise (a) melodic line(s) against it. (In addition to the manuscript paper that follows, if necessary, use the manuscript paper provided at the back of the book.)

2. Using the forms, devices, and techniques found in Bartók's music (*Examples 46–49*), write and perform several short compositions.

3. Study the examples of Bartók listed in the index of *MTTM*.

Mikrokosmos, No. 78

Béla Bartók

Example 49

MIKROKOSMOS
No. 86

Béla Bartók
(1881–1945)

Terms and Concepts

In your own words, define the following *Terms and Concepts*. When necessary, refer to the *Glossary* at the back of the book.

Bichord

Bitonality

Cadence

Counterpoint, invertible

Inversion, melodic

Melodic sequence

Mirror writing

Motive

Ostinato

Pedal point

Repetition

Tonal center

Study Questions

1. Define all of the performance instructions.

2. Analyze the melodic materials in each hand. What tonal center is conveyed in the right hand? in the left hand? What term best describes this tonal organization? How does the final cadence confirm this organization? (See *Information Bank, Topic 3*.)

3. There is a gradual increase in intensity beginning with *Più andante* and concluding at the "Tempo I" direction. How is this increase achieved? (See *Information Bank, Topic 8.*)

4. Locate the following devices in this composition:
   (a) Pedal point
   (b) Motive repetition and variation
   (c) Ostinato
   (d) Melodic sequence

5. Explain how mirror writing characterizes the middle voices in measures 27–31.

6. Compare measures 1–3 with measures 5–7. How do the devices of invertible counterpoint and melodic inversion apply?

Additional Activities

1. Write and perform a short two-part composition using a different scale in each part. (In addition to the manuscript paper that follows, if necessary, use the manuscript paper provided at the back of the book.)

2. Using the forms, devices, and techniques found in Bartók's music (see *Examples 46–49*), write and perform several short compositions.

3. Study the examples of Bartók listed in the index of *MTTM*.

Mikrokosmos, No. 86

Béla Bartók

[1 min. 18 sec]

Example 50
THE FIVE FINGERS
Lento

Igor Stravinsky
(1882–1971)

Terms and Concepts

In your own words, define the following *Terms and Concepts*. When necessary, refer to the *Glossary* at the back of the book.

Bimodality

Binary form

Bitonality

Canon

Imitation

Interval contraction

Interval expansion

Melodic sequence

Meter, mixed

Ostinato

Pedal point

Polymeter

Repetition

Ternary form

Tonal center

Study Questions

1. What is the prevailing tonal center of the composition? (See *Information Bank, Topic 3.*)

2. Which scale is used in the right hand? in the left hand? What term best describes the relationship between them?

3. Is the given $\frac{3}{4}$ meter conveyed consistently? If not, which meters are suggested by the phrasing in the left hand? in the right hand? Compare the metric organization of the two parts. What term best describes this relationship?

4. What device is used in the left hand of measures 9–13? Locate the use of this device in *Example 48*.

5. Discuss how the opening melodic idea in measures 1–2 of the right hand is developed throughout the composition.

6. What is the form of the entire composition? How is it determined? (See *Information Bank, Topics 4–5*.)

Additional Activities

1. Compose an ostinato pattern. Write (or improvise) and perform a melody against it. (In addition to the manuscript paper that follows, if necessary, use the manuscript paper provided at the back of the book.)

2. Write and perform a short composition that demonstrates bimodality.

3. Study the examples of Stravinsky listed in the index of *MTTM*.

The Five Fingers
Lento

Igor Stravinsky

Example 51
24 EASY PIANO PIECES FOR CHILDREN
"The Clown"

Dmitri Kabalevsky
(1904–87)

Terms and Concepts

In your own words, define the following *Terms and Concepts*. When necessary, refer to the *Glossary* at the back of the book.

Bimodality

Binary form

Change of mode

Form

Rondo form

Ternary form

Tonal center

Study Questions

1. What is the overall tonal center of this composition? How is it determined? (See *Information Bank, Topic 3.*)

2. What tonal center is conveyed in measures 9–12?

3. The melodic material presented in measures 1–8 uses pitches from both the major and minor scales. Explain. Is this same procedure used elsewhere in the composition?

4. What is the form of the entire composition? How is it determined? (See *Information Bank, Topics 4–5.*)

24 Easy Piano Pieces for Children
"The Clown"

Dmitri Kabalevsky

Example 52

Six Children's Pieces
"The Mechanical Doll"

Dmitri Shostakovich
(1906–75)

Terms and Concepts

In your own words, define the following *Terms and Concepts*. When necessary, refer to the *Glossary* at the back of the book.

Binary form

Canon

Counterpoint, invertible

Imitation

Melodic sequence

Motive

Pedal point

Repetition

Ternary form

Tonal center

Study Questions

1. What is the overall tonal center of this composition? How is it determined? What other tonal centers are conveyed? (See *Information Bank, Topic 3.*)

2. What is the overall form of this composition? How is it determined? (See *Information Bank, Topics 4–5.*)

3. Compare measures 1–4 with measures 30–33. What contrapuntal device is used?

4. What melodic/rhythmic motives give unity to this composition? (See *Information Bank, Topic 2.*)

Six Children's Pieces
"The Mechanical Doll"

Dmitri Shostakovich

300 • Example 52. *Six Children's Pieces*, Shostakovich

Example 53
MUSIC FOR CHILDREN
Op. 65
March

Sergei Prokofiev
(1891–1953)

Terms and Concepts

In your own words, define the following *Terms and Concepts*. When necessary, refer to the *Glossary* at the back of the book.

Cadence

Form

Motive

Pedal point

Phrase

Seventh chord

Tonal center

Tone cluster

Triad

Study Questions

1. Which tonal centers are used in this composition? (See *Information Bank, Topic 3.*)

2. Discuss the use of pedal points in this composition. How does each pedal point help to establish a tonal center? How does each help to provide unity? Locate the use of this device in *Examples 40, 45, 49,* and *55.*

3. The composition can be divided into four sections. What factors contribute to this sectionalization? (See *Information Bank, Topics 4–5.*)

4. How are the four sections of the composition related to one another? In what ways are they similar? How are they different from one another?

5. Review the organizational procedures of tonal harmony as used in compositions such as *Examples 15–21.* In what ways does *Example 53* reflect the chord vocabulary, root movements, and cadential procedures associated with those examples?

Music for Children, Op. 65
March

Sergei Prokofiev

• Example 53. *Music for Children*, Op. 65, Prokofiev

Example 54

PRELUDE AND FUGUE
ON A
THEME OF VITTORIA

Benjamin Britten
(1913–76)

Terms and Concepts

In your own words, define the following *Terms and Concepts*. When necessary, refer to the *Glossary* at the back of the book.

Answer

Augmentation

Canon

Counterpoint

Countersubject

Episode

Exposition

Fragmentation

Fugue

Imitation

Inversion, melodic

Melodic sequence

Motive

Pedal point

Prelude

Recitative

Repetition

Stretto

Subject

Tonal center

Study Questions

1. This prelude and fugue for organ is based on a melody from *Ecce Sacerdos Magnus*, a four-voice motet by the Renaissance Spanish composer Tomas de Victoria (ca. 1549–1611). The Italianized form of his name, Vittoria, was used by Benjamin Britten in the title of his composition. The motet melody follows.

Ec - ce sa - cer-dos mag - - nus

2. What is the overall tonal center of the prelude? of the fugue? (See *Information Bank, Topic 3.*)

3. An important motive in the prelude is found on beat 1 of measure 1. Is it related to the motet melody cited in Question 1? Trace the use of this motive throughout the prelude.

4. Several compositional devices are used in the prelude. Locate and identify the following:
   (a) Augmentation
   (b) Canon
   (c) Fragmentation
   (d) Imitation
   (e) Repetition
   (f) Melodic sequence

5. Compare this prelude with that of *Example 24*. Which general features are the same in both?

6. Compare this prelude with the recitative of *Example 13*. Which general features are the same in both?

7. Identify the subject of the fugue. Is it related to the motet melody cited in Question 1? Locate each statement of the subject in the fugue.

8. Locate and provide the measures of each exposition and each episode in the fugue.

9. Study the material that accompanies each statement of the subject. Is a countersubject used in the initial exposition? in subsequent expositions?

10. Where in the fugue is the subject stated in inversion? Where is stretto used? Locate each pedal point.

11. Three important motives of the fugue are initially presented in the subject, one each, respectively, in measures 1–3. Trace the use of these three motives throughout the fugue in melodic lines other than the subject.

12. The point of greatest intensity in the fugue is attained in measure 74. What musical factors contribute to the increasing momentum and direction culminating in measure 74? (See *Information Bank, Topics 7–8.*) How is the intensity dissipated after measure 74?

13. Compare the fugal procedures followed in this fugue with those in the fugue of *Example 24.*

Additional Activities

1. In a style of your choice, write a short composition that demonstrates inversion and stretto. (In addition to the manuscript paper that follows, if necessary, use the manuscript paper provided at the back of the book.)

2. Study other twentieth-century fugues in *AAM* and *BURK.*

3. Read and discuss Chapter 7, "Form in Twentieth-Century Music," in *MTTM.*

Prelude and Fugue
on a Theme of Vittoria

Benjamin Britten

314 • Example 54. *Prelude and Fugue on a Theme of Vittoria,* Britten

316 • Example 54. *Prelude and Fugue on a Theme of Vittoria*, Britten

Example 55

TWELVE POEMS
OF *EMILY DICKINSON*
No. 3, "Why Do They
Shut Me Out of Heaven?"

Aaron Copland
(1900–90)

Terms and Concepts

In your own words, define the following *Terms and Concepts*. When necessary, refer to the *Glossary* at the back of the book.

Added-note technique

Interval

Pedal point

Quartal harmony

Recitative

Text painting

Study Questions

1. How is the style of this composition influenced by recitative? (See *Example 13*.)

2. Discuss the use of the B♭ half note in measures 8–12 as a pedal point, a chord member, and an added note. Locate other uses of pedal point and added-note technique in this composition.

3. In measure 16, beats 1–3, the sonority can be analyzed as a quartal chord (G, C, F, B♭, and E♭). Locate other possible uses of quartal harmony in this composition.

4. Locate examples of quartal melodic writing in the voice part of this composition.

5. The harmonic interval of a minor seventh is used initially in measure 3. Trace its use as a unifying element throughout the composition.

6. Locate examples of text painting in the composition. (See also *Examples 13, 34,* and *37.*)

7. Define all of the performance instructions. Do these instructions help with the interpretation of this text?

Additional Activities

1. Study other compositions by Copland in *AAM* and *BURK.*

2. Write a composition in ternary form in which the A-sections use quartal harmony. Use the harmonic organization of your choice in the B-section. (In addition to the manuscript paper that follows, if necessary, use the manuscript paper provided at the back of the book.)

3. Read and discuss Chapter 3, "The Vertical Dimension: Chords and Simultaneities," in *MTTM.*

Twelve Poems of Emily Dickinson
No. 3, "Why Do They Shut Me Out of Heaven?"

Aaron Copland

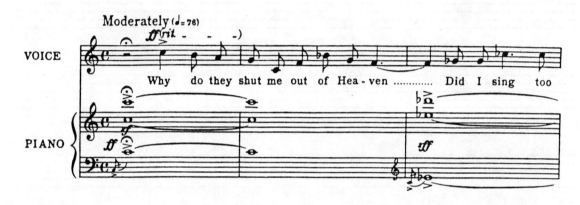

trou-bled them.... But don't shut the door, don't shut the door.........

.... Oh if I were the gen-tle-men in the

white robes and they were the lit-tle hand that knocked,......................

Could I for-bid, could I for-bid, could I for - bid.............

Why do they shut me out of Hea - ven,........ Did I sing too loud?....

Example 56
SONATA FOR VIOLIN
No. 2
Third Movement, "The Revival"

Charles Ives
(1874–1954)

Terms and Concepts

In your own words, define the following *Terms and Concepts*. When necessary, refer to the *Glossary* at the back of the book.

Bichord

Canon

Imitation

Meter

Ostinato

Pandiatonicism

Pedal point

Pentatonic scale

Polymeter

Polytonality

Quartal harmony

Quintal harmony

Tone cluster

Variation forms

Whole-tone scale

Study Questions

1. This movement is based on the hymn melody "Come, Thou Fount of Every Blessing," which follows. Trace the use of this melody throughout the movement.

Come, Thou Fount of Every Blessing

John Wyeth, 1812

2. The hymn melody is treated imitatively at the beginning of measure 15. Where else is it treated imitatively?

3. Beginning with measure 34, which meter is conveyed by the violin part? by the piano part? What term best describes this metric organization? Where else is this technique used? (See *Example 50.*)

4. Locate the following in *Example 56*:
   (a) Bichord
   (b) Whole-tone scale
   (c) Pentatonic scale
   (d) Polytonality
   (e) Pandiatonicism

(f) Quartal and quintal harmony

(g) Pedal point

(h) Tone cluster

(i) Ostinato

5. What is the form of the entire movement? (See *Information Bank, Topics 4–5.*) What factors create sectionalization? Compare this composition with *Example 29.*

6. Compare the use of tone clusters in this composition with their use in *Example 53.*

7. Which section of the movement is the most dramatic? (See *Information Bank, Topic 8.*) How is the musical intensity increased, then maintained, and finally dissipated?

Additional Activities

1. Write a short composition using one or more of the compositional devices listed under *Terms and Concepts* for this example. (In addition to the manuscript paper that follows, if necessary, use the manuscript paper provided at the back of the book.)

2. Listen to other compositions by Ives, such as his songs and his *Three Places in New England.* Discuss their stylistic features.

3. Study the compositions of Ives listed in the index of *MTTM.*

Sonata for Violin, No. 2
Third Movement, "The Revival"

Charles Ives

Example 57

DIVERTIMENTO FOR BAND

Prologue (Mm. 1–24)

Vincent Persichetti

(1915–87)

Terms and Concepts

In your own words, define the following *Terms and Concepts*. When necessary, refer to the *Glossary* at the back of the book.

Bichord

Bitonality

Eleventh chord

Ninth chord

Polychord

Seventh chord

Texture

Thirteenth chord

Timbre

Triad

Study Questions

1. After studying the score and listening to a performance of this composition, identify the instruments used in *Example 57*.

2. In measure 1, is the brass sonority heard as two separate triads (a bichord) or as a single ninth chord? Is the woodwind line heard there as part of the brass sonority, or does it convey a different tonal center?

3. Discuss the effect that timbre, spacing, rhythmic similarities, and texture have on the establishment and aural perception of different simultaneous triads. Compare measures 1–2 with measures 9–10.

4. How are the superimposed triads in measures 9–10 related to one another? Analyze them visually as a single sonority (a thirteenth chord) and also as a polychord. Which analysis can be aurally corroborated?

Additional Activities

1. Write and perform a short composition demonstrating the use of bichords. (In addition to the manuscript paper that follows, if necessary, use the manuscript paper provided at the back of the book.)

2. Read and discuss Chapter 3, "The Vertical Dimension: Chords and Simultaneities," in *MTTM*.

Divertimento for Band
Prologue (Measures 1–24)

Vincent Persichetti

• Example 57. *Divertimento for Band*, Persichetti

Example 58
TAR RIVER BLUES

Joseph Distefano
(1936–)

Terms and Concepts

In your own words, define the following *Terms and Concepts*. When necessary, refer to the *Glossary* at the back of the book.

Accent

Cadence

Contour

Dissonance

Dynamics

Form

Improvisation

Inversion, harmonic

Melodic sequence

Melody

Meter

Motive

Nonchord tone

Ostinato

Phrase

Popular chord symbols

Range

Repetition

Rhythm

Secondary chord

Seventh chord

Tempo

Tessitura

Texture

Tonal center

Triad

Twelve-bar blues

Variations forms

Study Questions

1. Compare the stylistic features of these melodies with those in *Examples 1–5, 8–9, 15–16, 25, 35, 46,* and *60*. (See *Information Bank, Topic 2*.) What similarities do you find? How have melodic concepts changed throughout history?

2. Using Roman numerals or other appropriate symbols, provide a harmonic analysis of the opening twelve-bar blues based on the given popular chord symbols. Compare the root movements in this example with those found in *Examples 15–21*. How are they similar? How do they differ?

3. Study the bass line of this twelve-bar blues. What device is used in the bass line of measures 1–4? Is this device used elsewhere?

4. Identify the melodic motives used in this twelve-bar blues. How are these motives used in the ensuing variation? Locate the use of repetition and sequence in the melody.

5. Locate the use of syncopation in this composition.

6. In a theme and variations, each variation retains some aspects of the theme and varies others. Using the following list as a guide, analyze the theme of the composition to determine its individual characteristics:
   (a) Melody and its melodic/rhythmic motives
   (b) Bass pitches
   (c) Harmony
   (d) Phrases
   (e) Overall form
   (f) Overall key and, if used, modulation and change of mode
   (g) Meter
   (h) Tempo
   (i) Articulation
   (j) Instrumentation
   (k) Texture
   (l) Dynamics
   (m) Degree of rhythmic activity
   (n) Amount and types of dissonance
   (o) Dramatic intensity

7. Compare the variation (measures 13–24) with the theme. Determine which aspects of the theme were retained and which were varied or abandoned. For example, circle the melody and bass pitches used in the theme and trace their presence in the corresponding measures of the variation.

8. Besides retaining certain aspects of the theme, each variation will exhibit individual features that serve to differentiate it from the theme and from other variations. Which features give this variation individuality? Consider the list in Question 6.

Additional Activities

1. Write and perform, or improvise, another bass line for the twelve-bar blues. (In addition to the manuscript paper that follows, if necessary, use the manuscript paper provided at the back of the book.)

2. Write and perform, or improvise, a melody against the given popular chord symbols for the twelve-bar blues.

• Example 58. *Tar River Blues*, Distefano

Tar River Blues

Joseph Distefano

Example 59

A LITTLE DUET
(FOR ZOOT AND CHET)

Jack Montrose
(1928–)

Terms and Concepts

In your own words, define the following *Terms and Concepts*. When necessary, refer to the *Glossary* at the back of the book.

Augmented sixth chord

Binary form

Fragmentation

Improvisation

Interval contraction

Interval expansion

Melodic sequence

Motive

Popular chord symbols

Rounded binary form

Seventh chord

Ternary form

Triad

Variation forms

Study Questions

1. Assuming that the motive consists of the first six notes, trace its use throughout this composition. What terms describe its subsequent use?

2. What structural term best describes the overall form of this composition? (See *Information Bank, Topics 4–5*).

3. Using the popular chord symbols given above the melody, provide a chordal accompaniment.

4. Using the popular chord symbols in measures 11–18, compose or improvise a melody for your instrument (or voice).

5. Respell the chord in measure 17 as a German augmented sixth chord in the key of F major. Is this respelled chord then resolved in the traditional manner? Explain.

Additional Activities

1. Compose and perform, or improvise, a new melody against the chords of this composition. (In addition to the manuscript paper that follows, if necessary, use the manuscript paper provided at the back of the book.)

2. Construct your own chord progression and compose or improvise a melody against it.

3. Listen to a performance of this composition and others by Zoot Sims and Chet Baker on Columbia CD 46174.

• Example 59. *A Little Duet (for Zoot and Chet)*, Montrose

A Little Duet (for Zoot and Chet)

Jack Montrose

Examples 60–61
**SIX SHORT PIECES
FOR PIANO**
Op. 19; No. 5, No. 6

Arnold Schoenberg
(1874–1951)

Terms and Concepts

In your own words, define the following *Terms and Concepts*. When necessary, refer to the *Glossary* at the back of the book.

Accent

Atonality

Cadence

Contour

Dynamics

Form

Interval

Inversion, melodic

Melodic sequence

Melody

Meter

Motive

Phrase

Quartal harmony

Range

Rhythm

Tempo

Tessitura

Texture

Tonal center

Study Questions

1. Compare the stylistic features of these melodies with those in *Examples 1–5, 8–9, 15–16, 25, 35, 46,* and *58.* (See *Information Bank, Topic 2.*) What similarities do you find? How have melodic concepts changed throughout history?

2. Translate and define all performance instructions in both compositions.

3. In *Example 60,* to what extent are the intervals of a third (major and minor) and the minor second used as unifying elements? Discuss their use in the final cadence. What other factors provide unity?

4. In *Example 61,* identify the harmonic sonorities used throughout the composition. How do they provide unity?

5. Which harmonic sonority used in *Example 61* is also used in *Examples 55* and *56*?

6. In *Example 61*, to what extent do the bar lines provide unity? What is their main purpose? Compare the use of bar lines in *Example 61* with their use in *Example 64*. How does each composer avoid a regular metric pulse?

7. Is an overall tonal center conveyed in either *Example 60* or *61*, or would the term *atonality* better describe their harmonic language? (See *Information Bank, Topic 3.*)

Additional Activities

1. Read and discuss Chapter 9, "Nonserial Atonality," in *MTTM*.

2. Write and perform a composition using three intervals of your choice. (In addition to the manuscript paper that follows, if necessary, use the manuscript paper provided at the back of the book.)

• Examples 60–61. *Six Short Pieces for Piano*, Op. 19; No. 5, No. 6, Schoenberg

Six Short Pieces for Piano
Op.19, No. 5

Arnold Schoenberg

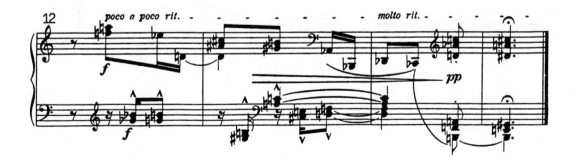

Example 60. No. 5 • **361**

Six Short Pieces for Piano,
Op. 19, No. 6

Arnold Schoenberg

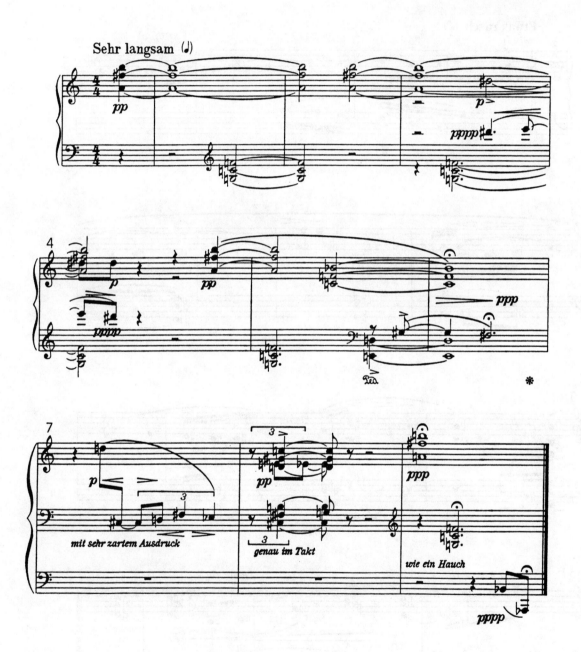

Example 62
SUITE FOR PIANO
Op. 25
Prelude

Arnold Schoenberg
(1874–1951)

Terms and Concepts

In your own words, define the following *Terms and Concepts*. When necessary, refer to the *Glossary* at the back of the book.

Contour

Dissonance

Dynamics

Enharmonic

Inversion, melodic

Matrix

Motive

Nonchord tone

Prelude

Retrograde

Retrograde inversion

Rhythm

Serial music

Suite

Tone row

Study Questions

1. A matrix for Schoenberg's *Suite for Piano*, Opus 25 follows:

Read across for Prime (P) →
Read down for Inversion (I) ↓
Read backward for Retrograde (R) ←
Read up for Retrograde Inversion (RI) ↑

364 • Example 62. *Suite for Piano*, Op. 25, Schoenberg

	I ↓												
→ P	e	f	g	db	gb	eb	ab	d	b	c	a	bb	R ←
	d#	e	f#	c	f	d	g	c#	a#	b	g#	a	
	c#	d	e	a#	d#	c	f	b	g#	a	f#	g	
	g	g#	a#	e	a	f#	b	f	d	d#	c	c#	
	d	d#	f	b	e	c#	f#	c	a	a#	g	g#	
	f	f#	g#	d	g	e	a	d#	c	c#	a#	b	
	c	c#	d#	a	d	b	e	a#	g	g#	f	f#	
	f#	g	a	d#	g#	f	a#	e	c#	d	b	c	
	a	a#	c	f#	b	g#	c#	g	e	f	d	d#	
	g#	a	b	f	a#	g	c	f#	d#	e	c#	d	
	b	c	d	g#	c#	a#	d#	a	f#	g	e	f	
	a#	b	c#	g	c	a	d	g#	f	f#	d#	e	
RI ↑													

In conjunction with this, study the *HDM* article, "Serial Music."

1. In what way is a single tone row of the matrix for this composition related to phrase construction? Which other musical elements delineate the phrasing? Consider factors such as:

   (a) Rhythm
   (b) Motives
   (c) Dynamics
   (d) Melodic contours
   (e) Performance instructions

2. Identify the important rhythmic motives and their subsequent variations (the repeated-note motive in measures 3–4, for example).

3. Notes 12, 11, 10, and 9 of the prime row spell BACH. (The pitch B♮ in German is *H*; see pitch 9 of Prime 1 in the matrix.) Of what historical significance is the incorporation of Bach's name in this genre? What unifying purpose within the composition do these four pitches (and their transpositions) have?

4. Examine the other preludes in this anthology (*Examples 24, 38–39, 45, and 54*). Are any general features present in all of these examples?

5. Does a twelve-tone composition use harmonic dissonance (passing tones, suspensions, and so on)? What is used in serial music to provide intensity, momentum, and direction? Consider factors such as melodic/rhythmic motives, dynamics, and contours. (See *Information Bank, Topic 8*.) Where in this composition is there an area that seems to require resolution (continuation)? What factors contribute to this need? What factors contribute to the sense of eventual resolution? Listen to this composition several times. Does the tone row provide the degree of aural unity analogous to a major or minor key? Discuss.

6. Discuss the ways in which *Example 62* is similar to *Examples 60–61*. On what factors do all three examples depend for unity and variety? (See *Information Bank, Topic 1*.)

Additional Activities

1. Write and perform a composition using the given matrix. (In addition to the manuscript paper that follows, if necessary, use the manuscript paper provided at the back of the book.)

2. Use a tone row of your own to construct a matrix. Using this matrix, write a serial composition incorporating some of the compositional devices listed under *Terms and Concepts*.

3. Read and discuss Chapter 10, "Classical Serialism," in *MTTM*.

• Example 62. *Suite for Piano*, Op. 25, Schoenberg

Suite for Piano, Op.25
Prelude

Arnold Schoenberg

Example 63
**CONCERTO FOR
NINE INSTRUMENTS**
Op. 25, First Movement (Mm. 1-27)

Anton Webern
(1883-1945)

Terms and Concepts

In your own words, define the following *Terms and Concepts*. When necessary, refer to the *Glossary* at the back of the book.

Concerto

Concert pitch

Inversion, melodic

Klangfarbenmelodie

Matrix

Motive

Repetition

Retrograde

Retrograde inversion

Serial music

Subset

Tone row

Study Questions

Begin by studying the *HDM* article, "Serial Music."

1. Translate and define all performance instructions, and name the instruments listed to the left of the music. (*Example 63* is a concert score; that is, all instruments sound as written.)

2. *Example 63* is based on the following tone row:

B Bb D   Eb G F#   G# E F   C C# A

Construct a matrix for this tone row on page 375. (See the matrix and instructions on pages 364–65.)

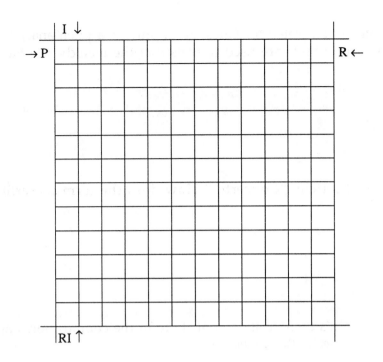

3. Discuss the intervallic structure of the four underlined subsets of the tone row given in Question 2. How do the subsets reflect the four forms of the row (that is, the original, the inversion, the retrograde, and the retrograde inversion)?

4. Identify the motive that dominates this excerpt. Trace its use and development.

5. How does Webern sustain the listener's interest despite the use of only one motive in this example?

6. Using the matrix completed for Question 2, provide a pitch analysis of *Example 63*. Discuss how the subsets are used to construct the melody, the harmony, and the phrasing.

7. Read the *HDM* article, "Concerto." How does the term *concerto* apply to this composition?

8. How does Webern's orchestration contribute to the composition's aural unity and variety? (See *Information Bank, Topic 1*.)

9. How does Webern use orchestration to increase the composition's intensity? What other musical elements does he use for this purpose? (See *Information Bank, Topic 8*.)

10. Compare *Example 62* with *Example 63*. Is the intervallic organization of Webern's serial music more discernible aurally and, consequently, is it a more cohesive aural factor than Schoenberg's intervallic organization? Discuss. What other similarities and differences do you find?

11. How does Webern's compositional process reflect and differ from the processes of composers such as Palestrina (see *Examples 10–11*), Bach (see *Examples 15–24*), Haydn (see *Examples 25, 28,* and *31*), and Bartók (see *Examples 46–49*)?

Additional Activities

1. Compose a melody, and orchestrate it to demonstrate *Klangfarbenmelodie*. (In addition to the manuscript paper that follows, if necessary, use the manuscript paper provided at the back of the book.)

2. Read and discuss Chapter 11, "Timbre and Texture: Acoustic," in *MTTM*.

3. Use a tone row of your own to construct a matrix, below. (See the matrix and instructions on pages 364–65.) Write a serial composition incorporating some of the compositional devices listed under *Terms and Concepts*.

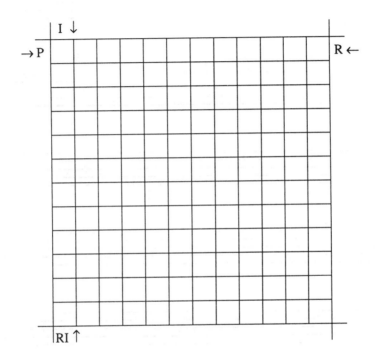

Concerto for Nine Instruments
Op.25, First Movement
(Measures 1–27)

Anton Webern

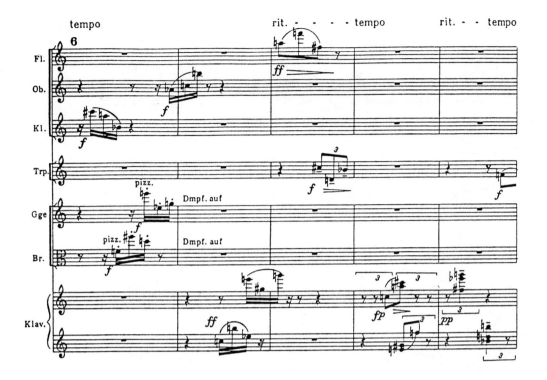

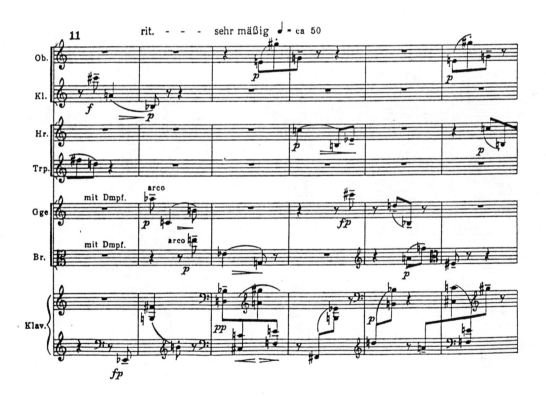

Example 63. *Concerto for Nine Instruments, Op. 25*, Webern

Example 64
STRUCTURES IA
Book I (Mm. 1–31)

Pierre Boulez
(1925–)

Terms and Concepts

In your own words, define the following *Terms and Concepts*. When necessary, refer to the *Glossary* at the back of the book.

Articulation

Dynamics

Matrix

Serial music

Tone row

Total organization

Study Questions

Study the HDM *article, "Serial Music."*

1. The tone row in this composition, which is borrowed from Olivier Messiaen's piano work, *Mode de valeurs et d'intensités* (*Mode of Time Values and Intensities*), is presented in measures 1–7 of the Piano I part. Construct a matrix using this tone row. (See the matrix and instructions on pages 364–65.)

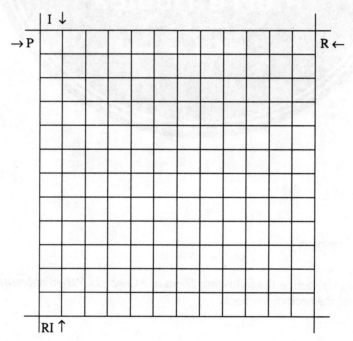

2. What form of the row is used in measures 1–7 of the Piano II part? What forms of the row are used thereafter in the Piano I part? in the Piano II part?

3. In addition to pitch, Boulez serializes other parameters in this composition: durations, dynamics, and mode of attack. The original durational series is formed by multiplying

a thirty-second note by the numbers 1 to 12. Which durational series is used in each piano part in measures 1–7?

4. To what degree does total organization provide aural unity? Compare the degree of aural unity in this composition with that in *Examples 62 and 63*.

Additional Activities

1. Read and discuss Chapter 13, "Serialism After 1945," in *MTTM*.

2. Write a twelve-tone composition in which a parameter in addition to pitch is treated serially. (In addition to the manuscript paper that follows, if necessary, use the manuscript paper provided at the back of the book.)

3. Write a melody that is primarily conjunct, and subject it to octave displacement. What effect does this have on the melody?

4. See the *HDM* article, "Pitch Names." Identify each pitch in measures 1–7 of this composition.

Structures Ia
Book I (Measures 1–31)

Pierre Boulez

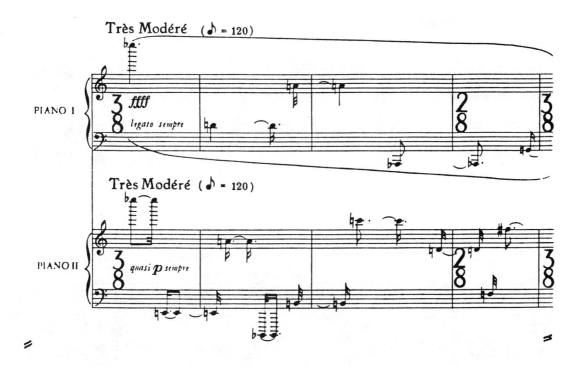

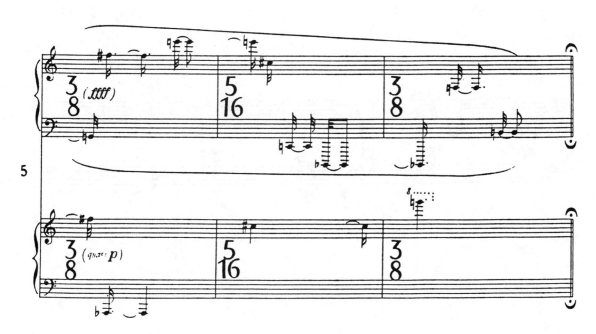

388 • Example 64. *Structures Ia*, Book I, Boulez

16

20

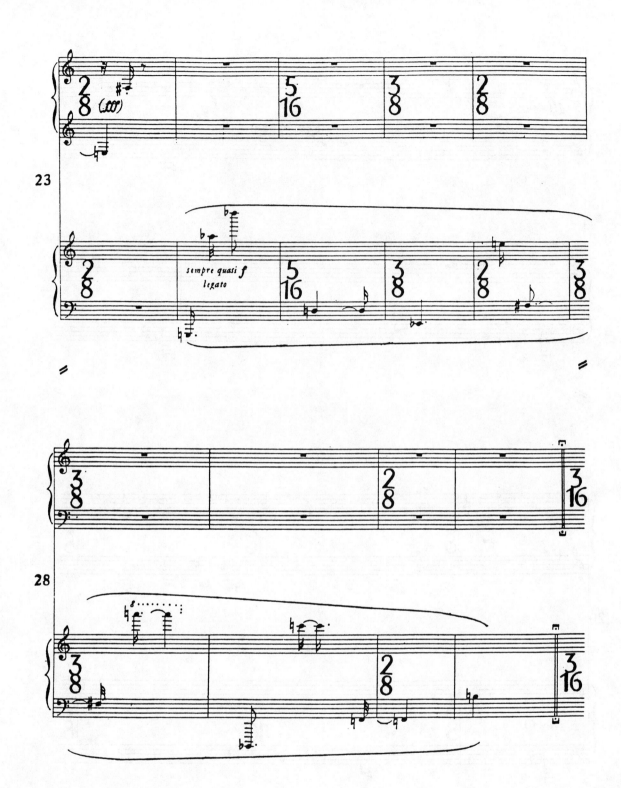

390 • Example 64. *Structures Ia*, Book I, Boulez

Example 65
PITCH CITY

William Duckworth
(1943–)

Terms and Concepts

In your own words, define the following *Terms and Concepts*. When necessary, refer
to the *Glossary* at the back of the book.

Aleatory music

Articulation

Harmony

Improvisation

Matrix

Rhythm

Texture

Timbre

Tone row

Study Questions

Study the HDM *article, "Aleatory Music."*

1. This composition is written to be performed by four wind instruments. The composer first constructed a matrix on a twelve-tone row (see *Example 62*) and then charted four different pitch routes, one for each performer. Two of the performers begin on the F♯ in the top left-hand corner; one plays F♯, E♭, D, F, and so on; the second plays F♯, A, B♭, G, and so on. The other two performers begin on the F♯ in the bottom right-hand corner, each also following a previously chosen indicated pitch path. The duration of each pitch is determined by the performer's ability to sustain each pitch as long as possible, breathing after each note. The composition ends when the last performer arrives at the concluding encircled pitch, F♯, in the middle of the matrix. The instruments need not end together. Perform this composition several times. If possible, record each performance, and then discuss the relative merits of each performance.

2. Discuss the role that improvisation plays in the performance of this composition. Consider parameters such as:
   (a) Rhythm
   (b) Timbre
   (c) Octave placement of each pitch
   (d) Harmony

(e) Texture

(f) Formal structure

3. How is the improvisation required for this example similar to that required for *Examples 58* and *59*? How is it different?

Additional Activities

1. Read and discuss Chapter 14, "The Roles of Chance and Choice in Twentieth-Century Music," in *MTTM*.

2. Using the matrix for *Example 62*, create your own compositions by charting pitch paths. Also, experiment by selecting pitches at random for a predetermined length of time. Which procedure is more successful? Discuss.

3. Create other aleatoric compositions, using the matrix, below, or one based on your own tone row. (See the matrix and instructions on pages 364–65.) Experiment by using various durations, dynamics, articulations, and octave placements for each pitch. (In addition to the manuscript paper that follows, if necessary, use the manuscript paper at the back of the book.)

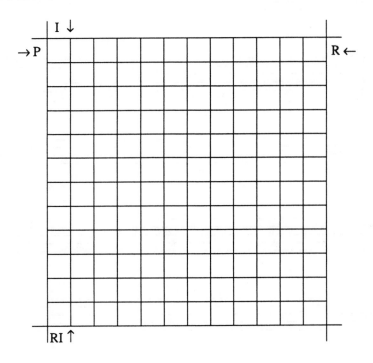

Example 65

Pitch City

William Duckworth

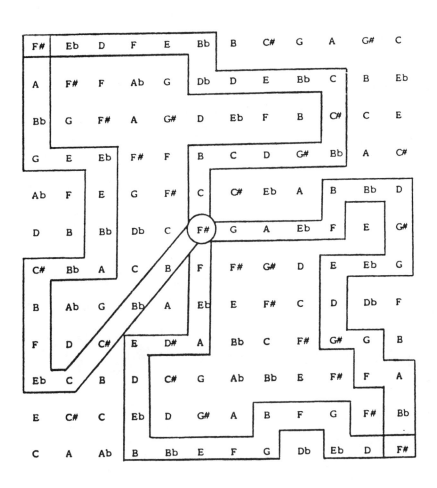

Glossary

accent: the emphasis of a pitch. (*See* Information Bank, Topics 3 and 7–8.) The four common types of accent are:

1. *agogic.* an emphasis caused by a longer rhythmic duration
2. *dynamic.* an emphasis indicated by symbols added by the composer
3. *metric.* an emphasis achieved by the meter, typically on the first beat of each measure
4. *tonic.* an emphasis created because a pitch is the highest note in a melodic contour

added-note technique: the twentieth-century practice of adding one or more pitches to a traditional sonority, usually tertian; for example, the addition of the pitch F to the C major triad (*C-E-G*). *See* Example 55

agogic accent: *see* accent

Alberti bass: a broken-chord accompaniment frequently found in keyboard compositions of the seventeenth and eighteenth centuries. It is named after the Italian composer Domenico Alberti (1710–40). *See* Examples 31–32; *see also* murky bass

aleatory music: the twentieth-century practice in which a composer consciously uses chance and unpredictability as a compositional or performance practice. *See* Example 65

answer: the restatement of a fugue subject at a different pitch level. An exact restatement is called a *real answer*, whereas a modified restatement is called a *tonal answer*. *See* Examples 24 (Fugue) and 54 (Fugue); *see also* countersubject, fugue, *and* subject

anticipation: *see* nonchord tone

antiphon: a class of Gregorian chant that stems from ancient antiphonal singing. It includes the Introit, Offertory, and Communion of the Mass. *See* Example 3; *see also* Mass

appoggiatura: *see* nonchord tone

aria: a dramatic solo composition for voice with accompaniment. It usually uses a text of reflection. *See* Example 13; *see also* recitative

articulation: the manner in which a note is initiated, sustained, or released; examples of articulation are slur, staccato, legato, and accent. *See* Information Bank, Topics 1–2 and 7

atonality: a term applied to twentieth-century music that lacks a tonal center. *See* Examples 60–65

augmentation: a compositional device in which a melodic/rhythmic idea is restated in longer note values. *See* Examples 46 and 54 (Prelude); *see also* compositional devices *for a list of other devices and* Information Bank, Topics 4 and 7

augmented sixth chord: a chromatic tertian triad or seventh chord that contains one diminished third. Traditionally, these chords function as altered secondary chords. (*See* secondary chords.) These chords are usually inverted so that the diminished third becomes an augmented sixth. (*See* Examples 19, 24, 31–33, 35, and 37; *see also* HDM.) The three common augmented sixth chords are:

1. *Italian sixth.* this chord is usually an altered IV chord in first inversion. In the key of C major or C minor, the pitches are F♯-A♭-C
2. *German sixth.* this chord is usually an altered IV7 chord in first inversion. In the key of C major or C minor, the pitches are F♯-A♭-C-E♭
3. *French sixth.* this chord is usually an altered II7 chord in second inversion. In the key of C major or C minor, the pitches are D-F♯-A♭-C

augmented triad: *see* triad

auxiliary: *see* neighbor tone *under* nonchord tone

ballett: an English Renaissance secular vocal composition. *See* Example 12

bar form: a two-part structure in which only the first part is repeated. *See* Examples 15, 20–21, and 34; *see also* Information Bank, Topics 1 and 4–5

basic duration: *see* beat

beat: the rhythmic value that receives one pulse; the basic time value as conveyed by one tick of the metronome. This rhythmic value may also be called the *basic duration*. *See* meter, rhythm, *and* tempo; *see also* Information Bank, Topics 6–7

bichord: *see* polychord

bimodality: *see* polymodality

binary form: a two-part structure, each part of which is usually repeated. This form is often used in dance music. *See* Examples 12–14, 25 (Minuet), 25 (Trio), 26, 33, and 36; *see also* rounded binary form *and* Information Bank, Topics 1 and 4–5

bitonality: *see* polytonality

cadence: a momentary or permanent cessation of the musical flow; the goal or culmination of a phrase. (*See* Information Bank, Topics 1–3.) The common types of cadences are:

1. *perfect authentic.* a V-I cadence in which both chords are in root position. The tonic chord must have the root in the highest part
2. *imperfect authentic.* any V-I cadence other than a *perfect authentic*
3. *half.* a cadence of temporary closure. This term is usually employed when a phrase ends with a V chord
4. *deceptive.* this term is usually employed when a phrase concludes with a V-VI chord succession rather than the anticipated V-I
5. *plagal.* this term is usually employed when a phrase concludes with a IV-I chord succession
6. *phrygian.* a cadence in which the tonic of the final chord is approached by a minor second from above and a major second from below. *See* Examples 7 and 10
7. *Landini.* a melodic cadential formula in which the sixth scale degree is inserted between the leading tone and the tonic—for example, the pitches *B-A-C*. The cadence, named after the medieval Italian composer Francesco Landini (1325–97), is heard in late medieval and early Renaissance music. *See* Example 6

cadential extension: a specific type of phrase extension used at the end of a phrase. It often features several repetitions of the cadential chords. *See* Example 31; *see also* phrase extension

cambiata: *see* nonchord tone

canon: a compositional device in which a melodic/rhythmic idea is strictly restated in a different part. *See* Examples 11, 22–23, 46, 54 (Prelude), and 56; *see also* compositional devices *for a list of other devices and* Information Bank, Topics 4 and 7

C clef: the clef that identifies the placement of middle C on one of the five lines of the staff. From the bottom line (1) to the top line (5) the placement is:

1. soprano
2. mezzo-soprano
3. alto
4. tenor
5. baritone

See Examples 1–3, 14, 43, and 63

chaccone: *see* variations forms

change of mode: a successive change of scale that retains the same tonic—for example, a change from C major to C minor. *See* Examples 28–29 and 34; *see also* modulation

character piece: a term used to describe the large repertoire of nineteenth-century short descriptive compositions for piano or for piano and solo instrument. *See* Examples 33, 35–36, 38–41, and 44–45

chorale: a hymn of the Lutheran Church. *See* Examples 15–21

coda: a section of music that is sometimes added either at the close of a composition or at the end of an extended section of a large structure (for example, the exposition of a sonata form) that serves to provide a further sense of finality. *See* Examples 26, 31, 32 (First and Third Movements), 37, and 41

compositional devices: *see* augmentation, canon, counterpoint (invertible), diminution, fragmentation, imitation, interval contraction, interval expansion, inversion (melodic), melodic sequence, mirror writing, ostinato, pedal point, repetition, retrograde, retrograde inversion, *and* stretto

concerto: a multimovement orchestral composition that features one or more instrumental soloists.

concert pitch: the actual pitch of the music as sounded by nontransposing instruments— for example, the flute and violin. Instruments that sound a pitch other than the one written are *transposing instruments*—for example, the B♭ trumpet and the F-French horn. *See* Example 43

consonance: a pitch that is a member of a given harmonic sonority and that therefore does not require resolution. Consonance is defined by the specific melodic/harmonic language of a given period of music or by the specific language of an individual composer. *See* dissonance

continuo: the supporting harmonies of a Baroque composition and the instruments that supply these harmonies (for example, a harpsichord or organ). These harmonies are improvised (or realized) from a given bass line and a set of figures and numbers for each chord below each note of the bass line. A melodic bass instrument (for example, a cello or bassoon) usually is used to reinforce this given bass line. *See* Example 14; *see also* figured bass

contour: the graphic shape of a melody. The concept of contour can be extended to the dramatic shape of a section of music or to an entire composition. *See* Information Bank, Topics 2 and 7–8

counterpoint: music of two or more independent, contrasting parts in which each part shares in the melodic presentation with near rhythmic equality. *See* Examples 6–11, 22–24, and 54; *see also* compositional devices *and* texture

counterpoint, invertible (*double counterpoint*): a contrapuntal compositional device in which two or more melodic lines are written so that any of these lines can be interchanged with any other and still maintain harmonic concordance. *See* Examples 24 (Fugue), 49, and 54 (Fugue); *see also* compositional devices *for a list of other devices*

countersubject: a secondary melodic/rhythmic idea that is sometimes used in a fugue. When a countersubject is employed, it is presented consistently against the subject and answer. *See* Example 24 (Fugue); *see also* answer, fugue, *and* subject

D. C. al fine: literally, "from the top (beginning) until finished." This term is placed at the end of a printed composition to instruct the performer to return to the beginning and repeat the music until the instruction *fine* appears. *See* Example 25

deceptive cadence: *see* cadence

development section: *see* sonata form

diminished triad: *see* triad

diminution: a compositional device in which a melodic/rhythmic idea is restated in shorter note values. *See* Example 54; *see also* compositional devices *for a list of other devices and* Information Bank, Topics 4 and 7

dissonance: a pitch that is not a member of a given harmonic sonority and therefore requires resolution. *See* Study Question 6 for Example 7 and Study Question 6 for Examples 8–9; *see also* consonance *and* nonchord tone

double period: four successive phrases that comprise a complete musical idea (both melodically and harmonically). *See* Examples 32 (First Movement), 33, 35, 37, and 41; *see also* period *and* phrase

dynamic accent: *see* accent

dynamics: the degree of volume, often indicated by words such as *forte (f)* and *piano (p)*. *See* Information Bank, Topics 1–2 and 8

eleventh chord: *see* ninth chord

enharmonic pitches: two pitches that are spelled differently but sound the same; for example, F♯ and G♭

episode: a section in a fugue that does not contain a complete statement of the subject. *See* Examples 24 (Fugue) and 54 (Fugue); *see also* exposition, fugue, *and* subject

escape tone: *see* nonchord tone

exposition: this term has two structural definitions:
1. a section in a fugue that contains at least one complete statement of the subject. *See* Examples 24 (Fugue) and 54 (Fugue); *see also* fugue *and* subject
2. a section in a sonata-form movement that initially presents the contrasting melodic/rhythmic ideas. The initial (*principal*) section of an exposition states melodic/rhythmic ideas in the overall tonic key of the movement; ensuing (*subordinate* and *closing*) sections most frequently state ideas in the dominant key if the overall key is major and in the relative major if the overall key is minor. *See* Examples 28, 31, and 32 (First and Second Movements); *see also* sonata form

fauxbourdon: literally "false bass." This term is used to denote successive triads in first inversion; a technique and style found in early Renaissance music. *See* Example 6

figured bass: a notational practice of the Baroque era in which the harmonies above the bass line are indicated by various figures and numbers. *See* Example 14; *see also* continuo

first inversion: *see* inversion, harmonic

form: the relationships among the elements of music (*melody, harmony, texture, rhythm, and timbre*) that result in the structural organization of a composition. *See* bar form, binary form, fugue, rondo form, rounded binary form, sonata form, through-composed, *and* variation forms; *see also* Information Bank, Topics 1–2 and 4–5

fragmentation: a compositional device in which only a part of a melodic/rhythmic idea is restated. *See* Examples 25 and 48; *see also* compositional devices *for a list of other devices and* Information Bank, Topics 4 and 7

French augmented sixth chord: *see* augmented sixth chord

fugue: a contrapuntal procedure or work that features one or more melodic ideas (*see* subject) in a series of imitative statements involving usually three to five rhythmically independent equal voices. *See* Examples 24 and 54; *see also* answer, compositional devices, countersubject, episode, *and* exposition, *and* HDM

German augmented sixth chord: *see* augmented sixth chord

Gregorian chant (plainsong): the monophonic liturgical music of the Roman Catholic Church. It is named after Pope Gregory, who reigned from 590 to 604. *See* Examples 1–3

ground bass: a repeated melodic line, often a phrase reiterated in the lowest sounding part, usually the bass, that serves as the basis for a set of variations. *See* Example 13; *see also* ostinato *and* variations forms

half cadence: *see* cadence

harmonic rhythm: the durational rate of successive chord changes. *See* Information Bank, Topics 6–8

harmonic sequence: the immediate restatement of a harmonic pattern at a different pitch level. *See* Examples 23, 24 (Prelude), 25 (Minuet), 30–31, 35, 39, and 41

harmony: two or more pitches sounding simultaneously. *See* Information Bank, Topic 1

homophonic texture: *see* texture

homorhythmic texture: *see* texture

imitation: a compositional device in which a melodic/rhythmic idea is immediately restated in another voice. It may be restated either strictly (*see* canon) or in modified form. *See* Examples 7–11, 14, 24 (Fugue), 46, and 54 (Fugue); *see also* compositional devices *for a list of other devices*

imperfect authentic cadence: *see* cadence

impressionism: a movement in the late nineteenth- and early twentieth-century French arts. Its primary representative in music was Claude Achille Debussy (1862–1918). *See* Example 45; *see also* HDM

improvisation: the performance practice of spontaneous composition, an essential feature of jazz. *See* Examples 58–59 and 65

interval: the distance between two pitches, either simultaneous (*harmonic*) or successive (*melodic*), as measured by the number of minor seconds (or half steps) between them—for example, major second (two minor seconds), minor third (three minor seconds), and perfect fifth (seven minor seconds)

interval contraction: a compositional device in which a melodic/rhythmic idea is restated using smaller intervals; for example, a fifth in the original statement may become a third in the restatement. *See* Examples 9, 26, and 48; *see also* compositional devices *for a list of other devices and* Information Bank, Topics 4 and 7

interval expansion: a compositional device in which a melodic/rhythmic idea is restated using larger intervals; for example, a third in the original statement may become a fifth in the restatement. *See* Examples 26 and 48; *see also* compositional devices *for a list of other devices; see also* Information Bank, Topics 4 and 7

invention: a short contrapuntal instrumental genre, usually employing two or three voices. *See* Examples 22–23; *see also* compositional devices

inversion, harmonic: the aspect of harmonic analysis that indicates which member of a chord is the lowest sounding pitch. (*See* seventh chord, tertian harmony, *and* triad.) The four common inversions are:

1. *root position.* the root of the chord is the lowest pitch
2. *first inversion.* the third of the chord is the lowest pitch
3. *second inversion.* the fifth of the chord is the lowest pitch
4. *third inversion.* the seventh of the chord is the lowest pitch

inversion, melodic: a compositional device in which a melodic/rhythmic idea is restated by using inverted intervals; for example, an ascending third in the original statement may become a descending third in the restatement. *See* Examples 9 and 54 (Fugue); *see also* compositional devices *for a list of other devices and* Information Bank, Topics 4 and 7

Italian augmented sixth chord: *see* augmented sixth chord

Klangfarbenmelodie: literally, "tone-color melody." A twentieth-century technique in which successive melodic pitches are presented by contrasting timbres. *See* Example 63

Landini cadence: *see* cadence

lied: a solo song written in German, usually with piano accompaniment. *See* Examples 34, 37, and 42

macro rhythm: the organization of *metric accents* (strong beats) as indicated by the given meter (*time signature*); for example, in $\frac{4}{4}$ meter the first and third beats are strong and the second and fourth are weak. This term is usually reserved for sixteenth-century counterpoint. *See* Examples 7–11; *see also* micro rhythm *and* Information Bank, No. 7

major triad: *see* triad

Mass: the ceremonial reenactment by the Roman Catholic Church of the Last Supper. As a music genre, it has come to mean a setting of five texts often referred to as the *Ordinary* of the Mass: Kyrie, Gloria, Credo, Sanctus, and Agnus Dei. *See* Examples 1–3 and 8–11; *see also* ordinary *and* proper

matrix: a "checkerboard" chart used in twelve-tone composition to display all forty-eight transpositions of the tone row:

      1. twelve prime rows
      2. twelve inversions
      3. twelve retrogrades
      4. twelve retrograde inversions

See Examples 62–65; *see also* serial music *and* tone row

mazurka: a Polish national dance that evolved into an independent composition for solo piano. It is in $\frac{3}{4}$ meter; it is performed at various tempos, from moderate to very fast, and features accents on either beat two or three. *See* Example 40

melodic sequence: a compositional device in which a melodic/rhythmic idea is immediately restated in the same part, but at a different pitch level. *See* compositional devices *for a list of other devices; see also* Information Bank, Topics 4 and 7.)

melody: an organized succession of pitches, rhythms, and, possibly, rests that forms a one-line musical entity. *See* motive, phrase, period, *and* double period; *see also* Information Bank, Topics 1–2

meter: a fraction-like number, such as $\frac{3}{4}$ or $\frac{6}{8}$ (often called a *time signature*), placed at the outset of a composition to define the rhythmic organization of a single measure. The bottom number usually identifies the beat (*basic duration*), whereas the top number usually identifies the number of beats per measure; however, the meter that is conveyed aurally will occasionally vary with the given meter. *See* beat, macro rhythm, micro rhythm, rhythm, *and* tempo; *see also* Information Bank, Topics 2 and 6–7

meter, mixed: changing meters (often referred to as *multimeter*), possibly in each successive measure. *See* Examples 43 and 64

metric accent: *see* accent

micro rhythm: the metric organization of a melodic line as conveyed by agogic accents. This meter may vary with the written meter (*time signature*). *See* Examples 7–11; *see also* macro rhythm *and* Information Bank, Topic 7

minor triad: *see* triad

minuet: a French national dance that evolved into an independent instrumental composition genre. It is in $\frac{3}{4}$ meter, performed at a moderate tempo, and is frequently in binary or rounded binary form. *See* Example 25 (Minuet)

mirror writing: a contrapuntal procedure in which a melodic or harmonic idea is presented simultaneously with its inversion. *See* Example 49; *see also* compositional devices *for a list of other devices*

modes, melodic: the system of scalar organization used during the medieval and Renaissance eras. *See* Examples 1–11 and 46–48; *see also* HDM

modes, rhythmic: the organization of rhythm found in the medieval secular music of the troubadours and trouveres. Each mode is based on the triple division of the beat. *See* Examples 4–5; *see also* HDM

modulation: a change of tonal center; for example, from C major to G major. (*See* change of mode.) Three common ways to describe a modulation are:

1. *common chord.* a diatonic chord in the former key becomes a diatonic chord in the new key. This chord is frequently called the *pivot chord.* For example, the I chord in the key of C major (C-E-G) becomes the IV chord in the key of G major
2. *chromatic chord.* the *pivot chord* is chromatic (nondiatonic) in either or both of the keys. For example, the II chord (V/V) in the key of C major (D-F♯-A) becomes the V chord in the key of G major
3. *phrase.* a phrase ends in a given key and the succeeding phrase begins in another key. No *pivot chord* is used

monophonic texture: *see* texture

motet: a sacred vocal composition other than a movement of the Mass. *See* Examples 6–7; *see also* Mass, ordinary, *and* proper

motive: a short melodic/rhythmic pattern consisting of at least two notes that is usually characterized by an accent. Because of its many transformations throughout a composition or section thereof, a motive serves to provide both unity and variety. *See* Information Bank, Topics 1–2 and 4–5

multimeter: *see* meter, mixed

murky bass: a broken octave accompaniment used in piano compositions of the Classical period. *See* Example 31; *see also* Alberti bass

musica ficta: literally, *false music.* This term is used in medieval and Renaissance music for pitches other than those of the diatonic mode. These nondiatonic pitches were originally added by the performer. *See* Examples 6–11

mystic chord: the mixed quartal chord C-F♯-B♭-E-A-D, associated with the music of Alexander Scriabin (1872–1915). *See* Example 44; *see also* HDM

Neapolitan sixth chord: a major triad constructed on the lowered second scale degree—for example, a D♭ major triad in the key of C major or C minor. *See* Examples 33, 35, and 42

neighbor tone (*auxiliary*): *see* nonchord tone

neumes: the notational signs of the medieval era. *See* Examples 1–3

ninth chord: a five-note tertian sonority formed by adding a ninth above the root; for example, C-E-G-B♭-D. This harmonic procedure can be extended to form eleventh (for example, C-E-G-B♭-D-F) and thirteenth (for example, C-E-G-B♭-D-F-A) chords. *See* Examples 38, 40, 42, and 57–58

nonchord tone: a pitch that sounds with a given chord but is not a member of that chord. The specific type of nonchord tone is defined by its linear approach (preparation), departure (resolution), and rhythmic placement. (*See* Study Question 6 for Example 7 and Study Question 6 for Examples 8–9; *see also* dissonance *and* Information Bank, Topics 6–8.) The eight common nonchord tones are:

1. *passing tone.* a nonchord tone approached by step and resolved by step in the same direction. It may be either diatonic or chromatic as well as accented (on a downbeat) or unaccented

2. *neighbor tone (auxiliary).* a nonchord tone approached by step and resolved back to the same pitch. It may be either diatonic or chromatic and is usually unaccented

3. *suspension.* an accented nonchord tone approached by the same pitch (either tied or rearticulated) and resolved down by step

4. *retardation.* an accented nonchord tone approached by the same pitch (either tied or rearticulated) and resolved up by step

5. *appoggiatura.* an accented nonchord tone approached by skip and resolved by step.

6. *cambiata.* an unaccented nonchord tone approached by skip and resolved by step

7. *escape tone.* an unaccented nonchord tone approached by step and resolved by skip

8. *anticipation.* an unaccented nonchord tone approached by either step or skip and resolved to the same pitch

nontransposing instrument: *see* concert pitch

ordinary: the texts of the Roman Catholic Mass performed at each service. These texts are the Kyrie, Gloria, Credo, Sanctus, and Agnus Dei. *See* Examples 1–2; *see also* Mass *and* proper

ostinato: a compositional device in which a melodic/rhythmic idea, often a motive, is immediately restated several times at the same pitch level and usually in the same part. *See* Examples 13, 48–51, 56, and 58; *see also* compositional devices *for a list of other devices and* ground bass, motive, *and* variation forms, *and* Information Bank, Topics 4 and 7

pandiatonicism: the twentieth-century technique of using only the pitches of a diatonic scale but without the traditional harmonic relationships. It is also called *white-note music. See* Example 56

passacaglia: *see* variations forms

passing tone: *see* nonchord tone

pedal point: a sustained or reiterated pitch. This compositional device is usually in the lowest part and at any given time can be a chord tone or a nonchord tone. This pitch sounds against contrasting melodic/harmonic material. *See* Examples 22, 24 (Prelude), 25 (Trio), 40, 45, 49, and 52–56; *see also* compositional devices *for a list of other devices, and* Information Bank, Topics 4 and 7

pentatonic scale: a five-tone scale, most frequently exemplified by the pitches C-D-E-G-A. *See* Examples 45 and 56

perfect authentic cadence: *see* cadence

period: two or more successive phrases that comprise a complete musical idea (both melodically and harmonically). Successive phrases or successive periods within a double period have either the same (*symmetrical*) or different (*asymmetrical*) lengths and contain either the same (*parallel*) or different (*contrasting*) melodic/rhythmic ideas. *See* phrase *and* double period

phrase: a musical statement that closes with a cadence. *See* period *and* double period; *see also* Information Bank, Topic 2

phrase extension: the lengthening of a phrase beyond the number of measures used in surrounding phrases. *See* Example 27; *see also* Information Bank, Topic 7

phrygian cadence: *see* cadence

pitch names: a means used to identify the same pitch name in different octaves. *See* HDM

pivot chord: *see* modulation

plagal cadence: *see* cadence

plainsong: *see* Gregorian chant

polychord: the twentieth-century technique of simultaneously using two (*bichord*) or more chords, usually tertian sonorities. *See* Examples 49 and 56–57

polymeter: the simultaneous use of two or more meters, either written or implied. *See* Examples 50 and 56

polymodality: the twentieth-century technique of simultaneously using two (*bimodality*) or more modes (*scales*). These modes can have the same or different tonics. *See* Examples 47, 49–50, and 56

polyphonic texture: *see* texture

polytonality: the twentieth-century technique of simultaneously using two (*bitonality*) or more tonal centers. *See* Examples 49 and 56

popular chord symbols: the signs and symbols used to indicate the harmonic accompaniment of contemporary melodies. This harmonic accompaniment is realized by a chord-playing instrument—for example, a keyboard instrument or guitar. *See* Examples 58–59

prelude: during the history of music this term has come to have three meanings:

1. an introductory section of a larger single-movement composition. *See* Example 42
2. the first movement of a composition with two or more movements. *See* Examples 24, 54, and 62
3. a single-movement composition. *See* Examples 38–39 and 45

program music: the practice of using melodic, harmonic, and rhythmic materials in an instrumental composition to suggest some extramusical idea, such as a literary work, an event in nature, or a psychological state. *See* Example 43; *see also* text painting

proper: the texts of the Roman Catholic Mass that vary at each service. These texts are the Introit, Gradual, Alleluia (or Tract), Offertory, and Communion. *See* Example 3; *see also* Mass *and* Ordinary

quartal harmony: a twentieth-century harmonic technique in which chords are constructed using intervals of a fourth. *See* Examples 44, 55–56, and 61

quintal harmony: a twentieth-century harmonic technique in which chords are constructed using intervals of a fifth. *See* Example 56

range: the span of notes from lowest to highest. This term may be applied to a single line of music or to an entire composition. *See* tessitura; *see also* Information Bank, Topic 2

recapitulation: *see* sonata form

recitative: a solo vocal style, often devoid of an inherent tempo, that reflects the natural pattern of the language in which it is written. It uses a narrative text, minimum accompaniment, and it often precedes the more elaborate and reflective aria. *See* Examples 13 and 55; *see also* aria

refrain: the repeated portion of a text, often consisting of one or two lines. These lines of text are usually found at the conclusion of each stanza. A refrain usually employs the same music at each repetition. *See* Examples 4–5; *see also* verse

repetition: a compositional device in which a melodic/rhythmic idea is restated in the same part at the same pitch level. *See* compositional devices *for a list of other devices*; *see also* Information Bank, Topics 4 and 7

retardation: *see* nonchord tone

retrograde: a compositional device in which a melodic/rhythmic idea is restated backwards. *See* compositional devices *for a list of other devices*; *see also* Information Bank, Topics 4 and 7

retrograde inversion: a compositional device in which a melodic/rhythmic idea is restated both backwards and inverted. *See* compositional devices *for a list of other devices*; *see also* Information Bank, Topics 4 and 7

rhythm: the principles of organization that regulate the durational flow of music in time. *See* beat, meter, *and* tempo; *see also* Information Bank, Topics 1–2 and 6–8

rondo form: a single-movement structure that features at least three statements of the initial melodic idea. These statements are separated by contrasting melodic and harmonic ideas; for example, ABABA, ABACA, or ABACABA. *See* Examples 4, 30, 32 (Third Movement), and 40; *see also* Information Bank, Topics 1 and 4–5

root position: *see* inversion *and* harmonic

rounded binary form: a specific type of binary form in which a portion of the beginning of the first section returns near the close of the second section. It is a structural ancestor of sonata form. *See* Examples 14, 25 (Minuet), 25 (Trio), 26, 36, and 59; *see also* binary form *and* sonata form, *and* Information Bank, Topics 1 and 4–5

secondary chord: a chord that functions as a dominant (V) or leading-tone chord (vii) to a tonal center other than the prevailing tonic (for example, V/V or vii/vi)

second inversion: *see* inversion, harmonic

serial music (*twelve-tone composition*): the twentieth-century technique in which a composer predetermines an ordering of pitches and intervals. *See* Examples 62–64; *see also* matrix, subset, tone row, *and* total organization, *and* HDM

seventh chord: a four-note tertian sonority that is formed by adding a seventh above the root of a triad. (*See* inversion (harmonic), tertian harmony, *and* triad.) The five common types of seventh chords are:

1. *major-major.* a major triad with a major seventh above the root (for example, C-E-G-B)
2. *major-minor (dominant seventh).* a major triad with a minor seventh above the root (for example, C-E-G-B♭)
3. *minor-minor.* a minor triad with a minor seventh above the root (for example, C-E♭-G-B♭)
4. *diminished-minor (half-diminished).* a diminished triad with a minor seventh above the root (for example, C-E♭-G♭-B♭)
5. *diminished-diminished (fully diminished).* a diminished triad with a diminished seventh above the root (for example, C-E♭-G♭-B♭♭)

sonata: An instrumental composition, usually consisting of three or four movements. Its development began in the Baroque period and continues to the present. *See* Example 32; *see also* HDM

sonata form: a three-part single-movement form in which the first part (the *exposition*) presents contrasting melodic/rhythmic/tonal materials, the second part (the *development*) manipulates these ideas, employing a variety of harmonic and melodic compositional procedures, and the third part (the *recapitulation*) restates these ideas. This definition outlines sonata form only in its broadest sense. Each movement in sonata form will exhibit its own individual characteristics. An introduction may precede the exposition and a coda may follow the exposition and/or the recapitulation without altering the basic three-part structure. *See* Examples 28, 31, and 32 (First and Second Movements); *see also* coda, exposition, *and* rounded binary form; Information Bank, Topics 1 and 4–5; *and* HDM

sonatina: a multimovement instrumental composition in which the individual movements are shorter and less complex than those in a traditional sonata. *See Example 28*

stretto: a compositional device in which overlapping restatements of a melodic/rhythmic idea are presented in close succession. *See Examples 24 (Fugue), 46, and 54 (Fugue); see also compositional devices for a list of other devices, and Information Bank, Topics 4 and 7*

strophic: a procedure in which each stanza of a text is set to the same music

subject: the primary melodic/rhythmic idea of a contrapuntal composition. This term is usually used when analyzing a fugue. *See Examples 24 (Fugue) and 54 (Fugue); see also answer, countersubject, and fugue*

subset: a segment of a tone row. For example, a twelve-tone row can be divided into two subsets of six pitches each. *See Example 63; see also tone row and serial music*

suite: a multimovement instrumental composition that consists of various dance-styled movements

suspension: *see nonchord tone*

tempo: the rate or speed of each beat. A tempo is often indicated by a metronome marking and/or a variety of terms such as *presto*, *lento*, or *moderato*. *See beat, meter, and rhythm; see also Information Bank, Topics 1–2 and 6–7*

ternary form: a three-part structure characterized by statement, contrast, and restatement. *See Examples 1–2, 5, 25, 35, 45, 50, and 52–53; see also Information Bank, Topics 1 and 4–5*

tertian harmony: harmony in which chords are constructed using intervals of a third. *See triad, seventh chord, and ninth chord*

tessitura: the average placement of a melody within the total range. *See range; see also Information Bank, Topic 2*

text painting: the practice of suggesting extramusical ideas contained in the text of a vocal composition. For example, a melodic line may ascend when the words *life* or *sunlight* are used and descend with the words *death* or *darkness*. *See Examples 13, 34, 37, 42, and 55; see also program music*

texture: the relationship of simultaneously sounding lines of music. For the distinctions between *counterpoint* and *polyphony*, see *HDM*. (*See Information Bank, Topics 1, 4, and 6–8.*) The four textures are:

1. *monophonic.* one-line music. *See Examples 1–5*
2. *homophonic.* one prominent melody with supportive accompaniment. *See Examples 15, 25, 28, 31, 35, and 37*
3. *homorhythmic.* each line of music shares the same or nearly the same rhythm, and the top line assumes melodic leadership. This texture is sometimes grouped with *homophonic* texture. *See Examples 15–21*

4. *polyphonic.* each line of music shares in the melodic presentation and each exhibits rhythmic independence. *See* Examples 6–11, 22–23, 24 (Fugue), 54 (Fugue), and 63

theme and variations: *see* variations forms

third inversion: *see* inversion, harmonic

thirteenth chord: *see* ninth chord

through-composed form: a structure characterized by nonrepetitive music throughout. *See* Examples 3, 6–11, 16–17, 19, 42, and 60–61

timbre: the distinguishing sound of an individual instrument or combination of instruments. *See* Information Bank, Topic 1

time signature: *see* meter

tonal center: the focal pitch of a given scale or mode, usually referred to as the *tonic*, to which the other pitches are related—for example, the pitch F in the F major scale.

tone cluster: a twentieth-century harmonic technique in which a chord consists of juxtaposed major and/or minor seconds. *See* Examples 53 and 56

tone row: the ordering of the twelve chromatic pitches used in serial music. *See* Examples 62–65; *see also* matrix, serial music, *and* subset

tonic: *see* tonal center

tonic accent: *see* accent

total organization: an extension of the melodic/harmonic tone-row compositional technique to include the prearranged ordering of such elements as timbre, rhythm, dynamics, register, and articulation. *See* Example 64; *see also* matrix, serial music, *and* tone row

transposing instrument: *see* concert pitch

triad: a three-note sonority. The four common types of tertian triads are:

1. *major.* a major third and a perfect fifth above the tonic (for example, C-E-G)
2. *minor.* a minor third and a perfect fifth above the tonic (for example, C-E♭-G)
3. *diminished.* a minor third and a diminished fifth above the tonic (for example, C-E♭-G♭)
4. *augmented.* a major third and an augmented fifth above the tonic (for example, C-E-G♯)

trio: a distinct second section of music that often follows a minuet. The minuet is usually restated after the trio, thus making the total composition a three-part (ternary) structure. *See* Example 25

trio sonata: a genre, usually associated with the Baroque era, that features two treble instruments (often violins) with an accompaniment provided by the continuo. *See* Example 14; *see also* continuo *and* figured bass

twelve-bar blues: a twelve-measure harmonic progression using the tonic, subdominant, and dominant chords to form the basic harmonic accompaniment for blues improvisation. *See* Example 58

twelve-tone composition: *see* serial music

two-part form: *see* bar form, binary form, *and* rounded binary form

variation forms: an overall formal procedure that initially presents in a relatively simple setting musical ideas that serve as the basis for ensuing variations. Each variation proceeds by retaining one or more of these musical ideas while modifying others. (*See* Information Bank, Topics 1 and 4–5; *see also* HDM.) The three common variation forms and the distinguishing features of each are:

1. *theme and variations.* the melody initially presented is modified in each variation. *See* Example 29
2. *passacaglia.* the melody initially presented is retained in each variation whereas surrounding materials are modified. This melody is often called a *ground bass*. *See* Example 13 (Aria); *see also* ground bass
3. *chaccone.* the set of chords initially presented is retained in each variation whereas surrounding materials are modified. *See* Examples 58–59

verse: the stanza of text, that is, the unrepeated portions of a text. *See* Examples 4–5; *see also* refrain

waltz: an Austrian national dance that evolved into an independent instrumental composition. It is in $\frac{3}{4}$ meter and is usually performed at a moderate tempo. *See* Examples 33 and 41

white-note music: *see* pandiatonicism

whole-tone scale: a six-tone scale based exclusively on the interval of the major second or its *enharmonic* equivalent, for example, the pitches C-D-E-F♯-G♯-A♯. *See* Examples 45 and 56

Additional Manuscript Paper

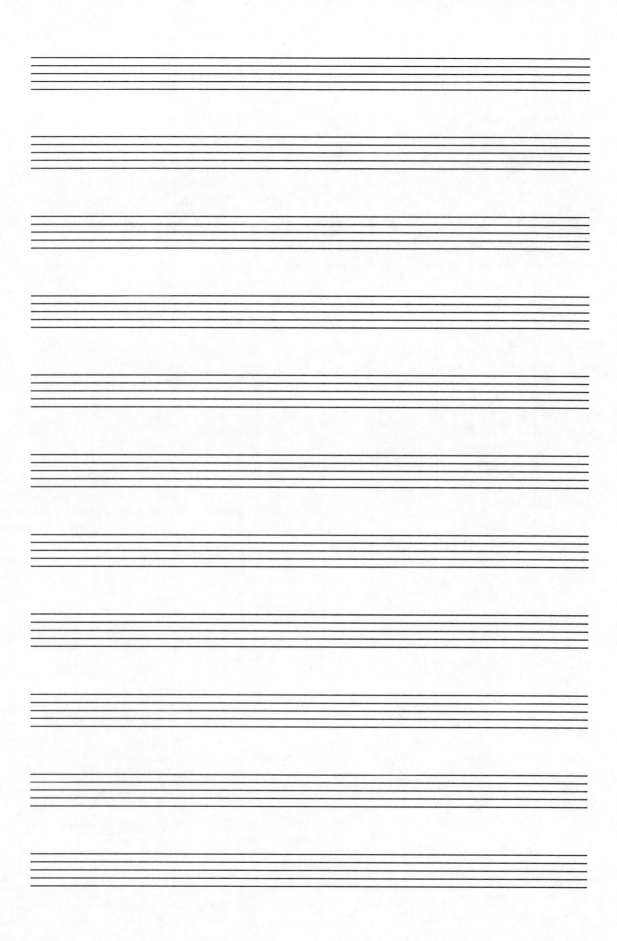

Information Bank

In answering the *Study Questions* for the various *Examples* of this anthology, the following topics should be considered:

1. Compositions often exhibit a judicious balance of unity and variety. Several musical elements that a composer can retain within a composition to achieve unity or can modify to achieve variety are:

(a) Melody	(d) Form	(g) Dynamics
(b) Harmony	(e) Texture	(h) Articulation
(c) Rhythm	(f) Timbre	(i) Tempo

    However, a single element can simultaneously supply both unity and variety; for example, a modulation from C major to G major provides unity by retaining the same scalar organization and provides variety by changing the tonal center. To maintain a balance between unity and variety, a composer can retain the features of one or more elements without any significant change while varying other elements.

2. Many basic stylistic features of a composition will be revealed through a thorough melodic analysis of the following factors:

(a) Contour	(h) Rhythmic organization
(b) Range	(i) Dynamics
(c) Tessitura	(j) Articulation
(d) Phrases	(k) Tempo
(e) Overall form	(l) Pitch materials
(f) Cadences	(m) Means of tonal organization
(g) Types of intervals	(n) Motives

3. The following factors contribute to the establishment of a tonal center:

    (a) The emphasis of a particular pitch at the beginning and the end of a composition
    (b) The cadences (melodic and harmonic)
    (c) The prominence of certain focal pitches through repetition, metric placement, and duration
    (d) The chromaticism
    (e) The use and organization of a particular scale or mode

4. The three basic principles of form are:

(a) Repetition	(b) Contrast	(c) Return to previous material

    Variation and development, two additional formal procedures, combine the principles of contrast and repetition in varying degrees.